I0832216

THE BIBLE IS ANTI-ZIONIST

40 REFLECTIONS ON THE GREATEST MORAL CRISIS OF OUR TIME

THE BIBLE IS ANTI-ZIONIST

40 REFLECTIONS ON THE GREATEST MORAL CRISIS OF OUR TIME

Jesse Steven Wheeler

Forward by Jonathan Kuttab

Friends of Sabeel North America

The Institute for the Study of Christian Zionism

THE BIBLE IS ANTI-ZIONIST
40 Reflections on the Greatest Moral Crisis of our Time

Friends of Sabeel North America (FOSNA)
Institute for the Study of Christian Zionism (ISCZ)
PO Box 3192
Greenwood Village, CO
80155
www.fosna.org | www.studychristianzionism.org

PAPERBACK ISBN: 979-8-9949297-3-5
SPIRAL BOUND: 979-8-9949297-1-1
EBOOK: 979-8-9949297-2-8
PDF DIGITAL: 979-8-9949297-0-4
KDP PRINT: 979-8-9949297-4-2

For:
my family,
near and far

CONTENTS

CONTENTS

TRANSLATIONS & PERMISSIONS

All prayers contained within are part of the weekly "Wave of Prayer" litany series, written and published by the Sabeel Ecumenical Liberation Theology Center in Jerusalem, Palestine: https://sabeel.org/category/wave-of-prayers/.

THE BIBLE IS ANTI-ZIONIST

FOREWORD: THE BIBLE ITSELF

FOREWORD

For a long time, Christian Zionists have claimed that the Bible not only supports but, in-fact, mandates their political agenda. By selectively quoting certain verses, frequently out of context, and ignoring most other relevant texts, they have laid claim to biblical authority while inserting their own political views and commentary as if it was gospel truth.

In the process, Christian Zionists have supported racist and oppressive policies, including fascism, colonialism, apartheid, and lately, even genocide, as if they were scripturally mandated. Opponents of Zionism and Israeli violence have been vilified as going against the will of God and the authority of the Bible.

This book reclaims the authority of Scripture by a thoughtful presentation that concentrates on the biblical text itself and invites the reader to prayerfully seek out its true meaning.

The results are amazing!

In my reading, it became abundantly clear to me that the Bible contradicts Zionism and is itself the best response to Christian Zionism. However, I invite you to engage with the content and develop your own conclusions.

Wheeler presents his readers with digestible passages of the Bible, each illuminating a specific topic along with a brief commentary relating that passage to the current situation in Palestine.

Then, he offers a relevant prayer from Sabeel's long-running *Wave of Prayer* series, together with a number of probing questions that help the reader (or discussion group) discover the true meaning of the Bible as it relates to Palestine/Israel and invites them to act accordingly.

Many liberals or progressives, when confronting fundamentalists and Evangelicals who support Zionism, often fail to impress theological conservatives because they either misunderstand or intentionally dismiss conservative appeals to "literalism" and Biblical authority. They then lose the argument by appearing to belittle, spiritualize, or "interpret away" those verses relied upon by Christian Zionists. They fail to use the most powerful tool at their disposal: the Bible itself.

Wheeler, himself coming from an Evangelical background with deep knowledge, respect, and appreciation for the authority of Scripture, offers the only true response to Christian Zionism: the biblical text, the message of which is truly anti-Zionist.

One example concerns the Zionist reference to Genesis 22, where God tells Abraham that "he will bless those who bless him and curse those who curse him and that through his seed shall all the nations be blessed."

Christian Zionists use this verse to garner support for the policies of the modern state of Israel, promising blessings to those who support Israel and curses to those who oppose it. The implication is that the modern state of Israel represents the "seed of Abraham."

A literal reading of Galatians 3:28, however, shows us that the Bible does not actually support such a view. Rather, it states explicitly that the "seed of Abraham" (used in the singular, not the plural) is used to refer to Christ himself through whom all the nations of the world are blessed. This is also consistent with the entire message of the New Testament that teaches that God's salvation and blessing is open to all nations, for "God so loved the world that he gave his only begotten son that whoever believes in him should not perish but have eternal life" (John 3:16).

This book of devotions not only reclaims the Bible itself and its message, but it provides a respectful invitation for readers to read, contemplate, pray, and make up their own minds about the issues. It is a useful tool for discussion in churches as well as individual contemplation.

I hope it will be used in many churches, particularly Evangelical churches who have for too long unquestioningly followed Christian Zionist teachings that are not at all biblical.

Jonathan Kuttab, Esq.
Executive Director, Friends of Sabeel North America
Author of *The Truth Shall Set You Free: The Story of a Palestinian Human Rights Lawyer Working for Peace and Justice in Palestine/Israel*

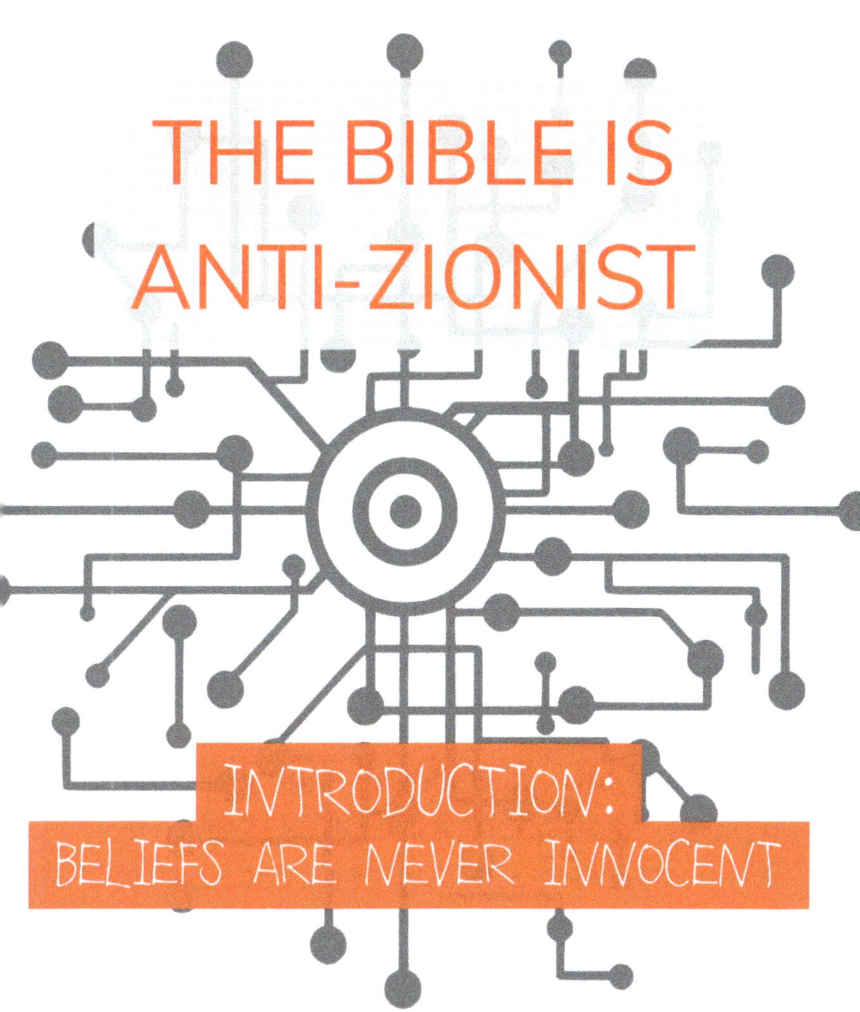

THE BIBLE IS ANTI-ZIONIST

INTRODUCTION: BELIEFS ARE NEVER INNOCENT

INTRODUCTION

> IN EVERYTHING, DO TO OTHERS AS YOU WOULD HAVE THEM DO TO YOU; FOR THIS IS THE LAW AND THE PROPHETS.

BEWARE OF FALSE PROPHETS, WHO COME TO YOU IN SHEEP'S CLOTHING BUT INWARDLY ARE RAVENOUS WOLVES. YOU WILL KNOW THEM BY THEIR FRUITS. ARE GRAPES GATHERED FROM THORNS, OR FIGS FROM THISTLES?

IN THE SAME WAY, EVERY GOOD TREE BEARS GOOD FRUIT, BUT THE BAD TREE BEARS BAD FRUIT. A GOOD TREE CANNOT BEAR BAD FRUIT, NOR CAN A BAD TREE BEAR GOOD FRUIT. EVERY TREE THAT DOES NOT BEAR GOOD FRUIT IS CUT DOWN AND THROWN INTO THE FIRE. THUS YOU WILL KNOW THEM BY THEIR FRUITS.

MATTHEW 7:12,15-20 (NRSV)

Beliefs are never innocent. In fact, within everything we think, say, or do can be found a variety of implicit belief systems, or "theologies." For theology (alongside its secularized twin —"ideology") encompasses our core beliefs as to how the universe functions and how we function within it.

Our theologies shape our identity and drive our sense of purpose, providing us with the interpretive lenses through which we find meaning in our daily lives. Moreover, they give shape to the moral values and ethical principles by which we relate to and live in community with others.

And, to repeat something I have shared many times over the years: some theologies are good; others are bad. But, in an era of "alternative facts," of "dual narratives" and "competing truth claims," how does one distinguish the good from the bad?

For the follower of Jesus, the answer is simple: FRUIT. "Watch out for false prophets," Jesus warns. "They come to you in sheep's clothing, but inwardly they are ferocious wolves. By their fruit you will recognize them." So, to distinguish between the true and false prophet, or anyone claiming to represent the will of God, Jesus simply declares: "By their fruit you will recognize them."

Likewise, to distinguish between a true and false moral-ethical, ideological, or political-economic system, one must examine the historical fruit of that system and ask:

- Does it lead us to love God, neighbor, and enemy as ourselves? Or, does it result in self-aggrandizement, or separationist and supremacist attitudes?

- Does it seek God's "kingdom come and will be done, on Earth as it is in Heaven?" Or, does it promote the idolatrous dominion of some other lord, pharaoh, flag, or financial system?

- Does it stand with the displaced, with the poor, the orphan, the widow, and the refugee? Or, does it produce harm?

Too often, we find walking the halls of power those false prophets who provide ideological cover for authority and its abuses, destructive wars, and the neglect, exploitation, and sacrifice of the world's most vulnerable upon the altars of profit and politics.

But, distinguishing good theology from bad theology comes down to this: ***good theology brings life; bad theology kills.***[1]

In her comprehensive treatment of the topic, Dr. Anne Perez explains, "Zionism is the view that Jews should have political, cultural, and national autonomy (self-rule) in part or the whole" of the Holy Land.[2] This sounds innocent enough, when devoid of context. But, to truly understand Zionism, Rev. Dr. Munther Isaac, Lutheran pastor, former Academic Dean at Bethlehem Bible College, and current Director of the Bethlehem Institute for Peace and Justice, asserts: "Zionism is what Zionism does!"[3]

And Zionism, over the past century, has resulted in a draconian system of apartheid, settler-colonial dispossession, and genocide. As observed within "the laboratory of history,"[4] the fruit of Zionism is death.

I recognize that for some, such a blunt, matter-of-fact depiction of Zionism—and Palestinian experiences of it—may be a shock. Others might wish to qualify or challenge my account. Yet, as stated in the new *Kairos Palestine II Document—A Moment of Truth: Faith in a Time of Genocide*, "We live now in a time of genocide, ethnic cleansing and forced displacement unfolding before the eyes of the world. This moment demands from us a new stand unlike any before it. It is both a decisive moment and a moment of truth."[5] The urgency of this moment demands intellectual honesty and moral clarity.

Unfortunately, people of faith have become the greatest cheerleaders, as well as political and financial supporters, for the evils of apartheid and forced displacement experienced by the Indigenous Palestinian people—the great tragedy being that many believe this is what the Bible commands. Thankfully, it does not.

Nevertheless, people are being hurt. They are being silenced, and they are being erased. But, it is often the members of "my own Christian tribe" who are the greatest proponents of Palestinian displacement, basing their support on a deeply misguided reading of the Bible and history. As such, I have a duty to respond.

For about two decades now, I have been outspoken in my support of Palestinian freedom. This, however, wasn't always the case, having been raised in a deeply Christian Zionist environment. The church culture of my youth was filled with end-times speculation and talk of the rapture, apocalyptic fantasies, "one-world governments," and right-wing politics. (Truth be told, such talk was rather traumatic for a child.)

Then, as a teenager, I met a woman. She is now my wife. She is a devout Christian. And, as it happens, she is Palestinian.

This simple fact catalyzed within me a paradigm

shift and life-long curiosity as to the history of Palestine, Palestinian Christianity, and the region as a whole. Inevitably, such a curiosity would foster within me an acute awareness of the historic injustices and violent realities faced by my family in Palestine.

Now, with some degrees in history and theology and life experience under my belt, including multiple years living and serving in the region, I am deeply anti-Zionist in my beliefs and my advocacy.

I want to be clear, however, that I still identify very much as an Evangelical Christian. I am "theologically orthodox" (i.e. affirming of the Nicaean Creed), committed to the Gospel of Christ, the Reign of God, and the Authority of Scripture. Whereas some instinctively apologize for or minimize the role of the Bible in their advocacy work—an understandable reaction to the frequent misuse and weaponization of religion—it was the Bible itself that converted me to the cause of liberation.

The more I read and the more I sought to follow after and adhere to teachings of Jesus, the more committed I became to the pursuit of justice and peace. Throughout this process, I have been delivered from numerous deeply harmful and problematic beliefs and ideologies, particularly those that propagate and provide ideological cover for the worst crimes and abuses of power imaginable—as we are witnessing today in Gaza, in East Jerusalem and the West Bank, in Lebanon, and throughout the region.

While I hope readers from any faith background, or none, might benefit from this resource, I acknowledge that am writing from an explicitly Christian vantage point—with all the implications and responsibilities entailed in this. As someone deeply committed to the authority of Scripture, questions of biblical interpretation are of profound importance, as are biblical ethics. So too are questions of history and historical interpretation, as we seek to respond faithfully to the reality of the situation as it exists "on the ground." If we are people committed to the truth, like we so often claim, then we must engage with the witness of both Scripture and history honestly and with open hearts, ready to be formed into the disciples God desires us to be.

Ultimately, a faith centered on Christ, formed by the self-sacrificial love of the cross, and committed to the reign of God, "on Earth as it is in Heaven," is a faith dedicated to personal and collective transformation. It is a faith dedicated to liberation, justice, and peace for each and every one of us, because each of us is beloved by and crafted in the very image of God.

A NOTE ON SOURCES AND INFLUENCES

This resource is not, nor does it claim to be a comprehensive theological examination of the topic. Neither is it is a detailed work of history or political analysis. Rather, it is a collection of short meditations designed to catalyze new ways of thinking about and responding to the greatest moral crisis of our time.

To facilitate ease of use as a practical resource, I have chosen to limit the use of endnotes within this collection. While the words may be my own (unless otherwise indicated), I am entirely dependent upon the witness of scholars, pastors, practitioners, activists, and persons of faith and conscience far wiser than myself. The phenomenal resources listed in the "Explore" subsections will point you in the direction of those voices on whom I depend.

I am especially indebted to the following: Martin Accad, Naim Ateek, the Awad family, Kenneth Bailey, Colin Chapman, Meindert Dijkstra, Havilah Dharamraj, Cedar Duaybis, Evelyne Reisacher, Ida Glaser, Munther Isaac, Jonathan Kuttab, Ussama Makdisi, Salim Munayer, Shadia Qubti, Mitri Raheb, Eugene Rogan, Stephen Sizer, Donald Wagner, and N.T. Wright. I owe a huge debt of gratitude to all of my Palestinian, Lebanese, and West Asian colleagues, friends, and family members, to the Friends of Sabeel community, and everyone who helped bring this project to fruition—near and far.

READ, REFLECT, PRAY, EXPLORE

The devotionals contained in these pages were designed with both personal and group study in mind, alongside a focus on simplicity and flexibility of use. As found, each meditation is organized according to a straightforward pattern of READ, REFLECT, PRAY, & EXPLORE:

- READ constitutes the bulk of a day's reflection, consisting of a particular passage (or passages) of Scripture followed by a short commentary on the meaning and message of the selection.

- REFLECT comprises three questions focused on a deep reading of the text, possible paradigm shifts and challenges, and a call to respond.

- PRAY is exactly that: a time for praise, confession, thanksgiving, petition, and intercession. Prayers were selected from Sabeel's weekly *Wave of Prayer*[6] series.

- EXPLORE contains a series of reading recommendations for those interested in pursuing specific topics in greater depth.

Now, having READ the Preface (including Matthew 7:12,15-20), I invite you to REFLECT, PRAY, & EXPLORE:

REFLECT

→ Prayerfully read through the verses one more time. Is there a particular word, phrase, or idea that captures your attention?

→ Is there anything new or surprising that you find in the passage? Do you find anything especially challenging?

→ Are you being called to respond or take action in any way?

PRAY

God of love, we confess our sins for all the ways we misuse your name and twist our faith to justify violence and oppression. Lord, help us witness your love by correcting all theologies which justify so much suffering and sin, and turn to theologies of love.

Lord, in your mercy, hear our prayer.

EXPLORE

Keeping the Faith: Reflections on Politics & Christianity in the Era of Trump & Beyond, edited by Jonathan Walton, Sy Hoekstra, and Suzie Lahoud

THE BIBLE IS
ANTI-ZIONIST
#1
THE HOLY CITY OF ZION

THE BIBLE IS ANTI-ZIONIST #1

ON THE HOLY MOUNTAIN STANDS THE CITY FOUNDED BY THE LORD. HE LOVES THE CITY OF JERUSALEM MORE THAN ANY OTHER DWELLING OF JACOB. O CITY OF GOD, WHAT GLORIOUS THINGS ARE SAID OF YOU!

I WILL COUNT EGYPT AND BABYLON AMONG THOSE WHO KNOW ME, ALSO PHILISTIA AND TYRE, AND EVEN DISTANT ETHIOPIA. THEY HAVE ALL BECOME CITIZENS OF JERUSALEM! REGARDING JERUSALEM IT WILL BE SAID,

" EVERYONE ENJOYS THE RIGHTS OF CITIZENSHIP THERE."

AND THE MOST HIGH WILL PERSONALLY BLESS THIS CITY. WHEN THE LORD REGISTERS THE NATIONS, HE WILL SAY, " THEY HAVE ALL BECOME CITIZENS OF JERUSALEM." THE PEOPLE WILL PLAY FLUTES AND SING, " THE SOURCE OF MY LIFE SPRINGS FROM JERUSALEM!"

PSALM 87 (NLT)

Jerusalem is afforded special status in the Hebrew Scriptures. As the location of the Temple—i.e. the dwelling place of God on earth and, therefore, the point at which Earth and Heaven converge—it is the "Zion" from which Zionism gets its name.

Known for generations in Arabic as *Al-Quds* ("The Holy"), its skyline has long occupied a central space in the iconography of the Palestinian movement. It is the Holy City of the Holy Land.

The location of Christ's death and resurrection is memorialized in the Church of the Holy Sepulcher, or *Kanīsat al-Qiyāmah* ("The Church of the Resurrection"), by Indigenous Palestinian Christians. Meanwhile, *Al-Aqsa* ("the farthest") Mosque is revered by Muslims around the world as the location from which Muhammad ascended to heaven on his night journey. As such, Jerusalem's status as the Holy City is only heightened.

YET, WHAT IS HOLY ABOUT THE HOLY CITY?

Psalm 87 gives us a clue.

For Jerusalem is the location from which God's blessing and just reign would flow out to encompass all nations and peoples on earth.

Over the centuries, it would in many ways come to resemble the diversity envisioned by the Psalmist. Today, as Israel enacts policies of ethnic exclusion and demographic homogenization, the Indigenous beauty, diversity, culture, and living history of the holy city are at serious risk of being lost forever.

Yet, it is precisely the Indigenous diversity, culture, and history that mark the city as holy—a holiness profaned by the evils of forced displacement, racial supremacy, and cultural erasure.

We must do what we can to save Jerusalem and preserve the true holiness of the holy city.

REFLECT

→ Prayerfully read through the verses one more time. Is there a particular word, phrase, or idea that captures your attention?

→ Is there anything new or surprising that you find in the passage? Do you find anything especially challenging?

→ Are you being called to respond or take action in any way?

PRAY

God of Peace, we lift our prayers for Jerusalem, a city sacred to many, yet scarred by division and domination. We give thanks for the work of Sabeel and all who labor to protect the dignity and diversity of this Holy City. As the powers of empire move to annex and erase Indigenous presence, we pray for courage to resist and wisdom to act.

Lord, in your mercy, hear our prayer.

EXPLORE

Nine Quarters of Jerusalem: A New Biography of the Old City, by Matthew Teller

THE BIBLE IS ANTI-ZIONIST

#2 WHOSE LAND?

THE BIBLE IS ANTI-ZIONIST #2

" [THE] FIFTIETH YEAR WILL BE A JUBILEE FOR YOU. DURING THAT YEAR YOU MUST NOT PLANT YOUR FIELDS OR STORE AWAY ANY OF THE CROPS THAT GROW ON THEIR OWN, AND DON' T GATHER THE GRAPES FROM YOUR UNPRUNED VINES . . .

" IF YOU WANT TO LIVE SECURELY IN THE LAND, FOLLOW MY DECREES AND OBEY MY REGULATIONS . . .

" THE LAND MUST NEVER BE SOLD ON A PERMANENT BASIS,

FOR THE LAND BELONGS TO ME. YOU ARE ONLY FOREIGNERS AND TENANT FARMERS WORKING FOR ME."

LEVITICUS 25:11;18;23 (NLT)

"To whom does the land belong?" is a question known to anyone familiar with the ongoing crisis in Palestine. Much ink and many hours have been spent exploring it, and much blood has been spilt pursuing an answer.

Colin Chapman's iconic *Whose Promised Land?* is a classic, yet ever-relevant work of history and theology. Another is Gary Burge's *Whose Land? Whose Promise?*

For his part, Israeli Prime Minister Netanyahu recently proclaimed, "There will be no Palestinian state; this land belongs to us!"[1] And in 2019, Israeli ambassador Danny Danon declared before the United Nations, "We have biblical rights to the land; the Bible is our deed!"[2]

In February 2026, U.S. Ambassador to Israel Mike Huckabee even spoke of Israel's "biblical right" to all land between the Nile River in Egypt and the Euphrates in Iraq, a sentiment quickly affirmed by Israeli opposition leader Yair Lapid. "I believe that our ownership deed over the land of Israel," he repeated, "is the Bible."[3]

Questions of ownership and occupancy are expected in situations of conflict. Yet, if scripture is to be consulted, then the actual words of the Bible must be examined.

And, as Leviticus clearly states, "The land belongs to God." So perhaps it is Palestinian Bishop Elias Chacour has the best book title when he proclaims: "We Belong to the Land!"[4]

As a sign that the land belongs to none but God, the Jubilee Year was to serve as "a massive reset," whereby all intervening sales were cancelled, all debts forgiven, and all bond servants released.

Furthermore, tenancy was contingent upon faithfulness to God's decrees, and failure to adhere to the terms of the lease was cause for eviction.

So, even if the Bible legally could function as a "land deed," it quite explicitly does not.

To be Zionist, therefore, is to violently assert squatters' rights over that which one has no authentic claim and to do so in flagrant disregard of God's decree.

REFLECT

→ Prayerfully read through the verses one more time. Is there a particular word, phrase, or idea that captures your attention?

→ Is there anything new or surprising that you find in the passage? Do you find anything especially challenging?

→ Are you being called to respond or take action in any way?

PRAY

Holy God, we come before you with heavy hearts as we witness the ever deepening of injustice in the land we call holy. Lord, you see the suffering of those who are displaced, injured, and grieving the loss of loved ones. You see the fear that grows as violence escalates, and the daily oppression faced by those living under occupation. We pray for protection for the vulnerable, courage for those who speak truth, and a turning of hearts toward justice.

Lord, in your mercy, hear our prayer.

EXPLORE

The Land Cries Out: Theology of the Land in the Israeli-Palestinian Context, edited by Salim Munayer and Lisa Loden

THE BIBLE IS ANTI-ZIONIST

#3

THE INDIGENOUS OTHER

THE BIBLE IS ANTI-ZIONIST #3

" DO NOT OPPRESS A FOREIGNER; YOU YOURSELVES KNOW HOW IT FEELS TO BE FOREIGNERS, BECAUSE YOU WERE FOREIGNERS IN EGYPT.

" FOR SIX YEARS YOU ARE TO SOW YOUR FIELDS AND HARVEST THE CROPS, BUT DURING THE SEVENTH YEAR LET THE LAND LIE UNPLOWED AND UNUSED. THEN THE POOR AMONG YOUR PEOPLE MAY GET FOOD FROM IT, AND THE WILD ANIMALS MAY EAT WHAT IS LEFT.

" SIX DAYS DO YOUR WORK, BUT ON THE SEVENTH DAY DO NOT WORK, SO THAT YOUR OX AND YOUR DONKEY MAY REST, AND SO THAT THE SERVANT BORN IN YOUR HOUSEHOLD AND THE FOREIGNER LIVING AMONG YOU MAY BE REFRESHED.

EXODUS 23:9-11 (NIV)

On the road to authentic and effective solidarity, a "rookie mistake" is to reach for passages like Exodus 23:9. Doing so can be incredibly harmful and insulting.

Overall, the command to protect and respect the strangers among us is quite beautiful. In pre-modern societies, to be a foreigner is to be without roots or resources, dependent entirely for survival on the goodwill of the local community. You are also a prime target for exploitation by corrupt employers or scapegoating by bigots and demagogues.

By keeping alive the collective memories of one's displacement, such commands are an essential precursor to the Golden Rule. They cultivate empathy as they lead us to "do for others as we would have them do for us." Zionism, as an ideology of Jewish supremacy, clearly fails this test.

SO, WHAT IS THE MISTAKE?

Like Native Americans, Black South Africans, European Jews, Armenians, Aboriginal Australians, and too many others, Palestinians have become the "Indigenous Other" in their own land.

In framing the Indigenous Palestinians as "alien and stranger," even if they are seen as strangers needing protection and welcome, we perpetuate an all-too-common settler-colonial sleight of hand.

"The othering of the Indigenous by calling them strangers," Rev. Dr. Mitri Raheb reminds us, "is an important feature of settler colonialism in which the natives are extraneous and the settlers are cast as natives."[1]

In describing the process of erasure inherent to western Christian support for Zionism, Raheb explains: "For Palestinians, including the Palestinian Christian community, Palestine is a real land with real people. It is our homeland, the land of our ancestors. For Christians in the West, Palestine is an imagined land they know mainly from the Bible. It has little, if anything, to do with the real Palestine."[2]

In fact, central to the Zionist project from its inception has been the violent imposition of a false construction of reality atop the lived, historically authentic Palestinian experience. It is an act of Indigenous erasure and a prelude to genocide.

REFLECT

→ Prayerfully read through the verses one more time. Is there a particular word, phrase, or idea that captures your attention?

→ Is there anything new or surprising that you find in the passage? Do you find anything especially challenging?

→ Are you being called to respond or take action in any way?

PRAY

Almighty Creator, we witness the many ways that hatred and racism seek to erase the rich diversity and social fabric of your creation. In the face of such evil, remind us that we must be steadfast in the movement of nonviolence, justice, and inclusivity. We "pray for the peace of Jerusalem" (Psalm 48:1-2) and for the transformation of hearts, that they may repent from their hatred and participate in the work of peace and justice in the Holy Land.

Lord, in your mercy, hear our prayer.

EXPLORE

Decolonizing Palestine: The Land, The People, The Bible, by Mitri Raheb

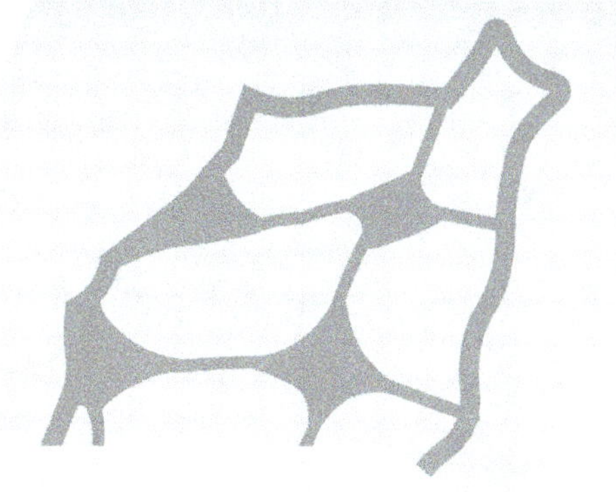

THE BIBLE IS ANTI-ZIONIST

#4 NATIVE BORN

THE BIBLE IS ANTI-ZIONIST #4

" DIVIDE THE LAND WITHIN THESE BOUNDARIES AMONG THE TRIBES OF ISRAEL. DISTRIBUTE THE LAND AS AN ALLOTMENT FOR YOURSELVES AND FOR THE FOREIGNERS WHO HAVE JOINED YOU AND ARE RAISING THEIR FAMILIES AMONG YOU.

THEY WILL BE LIKE NATIVE-BORN ISRAELITES TO YOU AND WILL RECEIVE AN ALLOTMENT AMONG THE TRIBES.

THESE FOREIGNERS ARE TO BE GIVEN LAND WITHIN THE TERRITORY OF THE TRIBE WITH WHOM THEY NOW LIVE. I, THE SOVEREIGN LORD, HAVE SPOKEN!

EZEKIEL 47:21-23 (NLT)

To reiterate what I shared previously, Palestinians are NOT foreigners.

As leading historian William Dalrymple tells us, "Palestine is a word as old as literacy itself. In the Egyptian form, it's '*Peleset*' in the hieroglyphs. The Assyrians talk about '*Palestina*.' Herodotus, the father of history talks about Palestine, saying there are Arabs where Gaza is. It's a long, complicated history of many peoples. The Levant is the most fantastically mixed, plural, and cosmopolitan part of the world. Every [seaport] has mixtures of people. And that's true of Palestine, too . . .

"There's migrations in and out throughout the whole of history, but there is always this group of people there. And the DNA of modern Palestinians is almost identical to the Bronze Age people. They are the same people."[1]

Modern Palestinians ARE the Indigenous inhabitants of the Holy Land: inheritors to the legacy of the ancient Canaanites, genetic heirs to BOTH Israelites and Philistines, and the descendants of myriad migrant populations and invasion forces throughout history.

In Palestine, empires have come and gone: Egyptian, Assyrian, Babylonian, Persian, Greek, Roman (and Byzantine), Arab, Crusader, Turkish, and British. But the people of the land always remained—until Zionism.

According to Scripture and history alike, the people of the land have always been comprised of a diverse and cosmopolitan mix of ethnicities, religions, and languages. Therefore, as Dalrymple states, Zionist attempts to "rob the Palestinians of their history and attempting to erase their ancient presence from the land is as reprehensible as actual ethnic cleansing."[2]

In light of this, an alternate reading of today's passage could be: "strangers are to share in the same inheritance as kin," accounting for the fact that multiple peoples have always shared the land, coming and going across time.

Ultimately, Ezekiel's restoration vision looks nothing like the Zionist pursuit of forced displacement, ethnic supremacy, and cultural erasure. Rather, the prophet offers an authentic and just vision of unity amidst diversity.

REFLECT

→ Prayerfully read through the verses one more time. Is there a particular word, phrase, or idea that captures your attention?

→ Is there anything new or surprising that you find in the passage? Do you find anything especially challenging?

→ Are you being called to respond or take action in any way?

PRAY

God of Justice, peace seems far away and the darkness is overwhelming. Yet, even when hope is low, we hold onto your call to resist the temptations of evil and domination. Forgive us for our complicity in systems of oppression that are obstacles to the peace you envision for us. Holy Spirit, give us the strength and courage to practice truth, fairness, and equality to all people. We pray for an end to all forms of hatred and violence and for a just peace to take root.

Lord, in your mercy, hear our prayer.

EXPLORE

Palestine and Israel: A Concealed History, by Meindert Dijkstra

THE BIBLE IS ANTI-ZIONIST

#5

THE WORLD & EVERYTHING IN IT

THE BIBLE IS ANTI-ZIONIST #5

BUT WHO IS ABLE TO BUILD SUCH A TEMPLE WHEN EVEN THE HIGHEST HEAVEN CAN'T CONTAIN GOD?

2 CHRONICLES 2:6 (CEB)

THE LORD SAYS: HEAVEN IS MY THRONE, AND EARTH IS MY FOOTSTOOL. SO WHERE COULD YOU BUILD A HOUSE FOR ME, AND WHERE COULD MY RESTING PLACE BE? MY HAND MADE ALL THESE THINGS AND BROUGHT THEM INTO BEING, SAYS THE LORD. BUT HERE IS WHERE I WILL LOOK: TO THE HUMBLE AND CONTRITE IN SPIRIT WHO TREMBLE AT MY WORD . . . I'M COMING TO GATHER ALL NATIONS AND CULTURES. THEY WILL COME TO SEE MY GLORY.

ISAIAH 66:1-2,18 (CEB)

GOD, WHO MADE THE WORLD AND EVERYTHING IN IT, IS LORD OF HEAVEN AND EARTH. HE DOESN'T LIVE IN TEMPLES MADE WITH HUMAN HANDS.

ACTS 17:24 (CEB)

DON'T YOU KNOW THAT YOU ARE GOD'S TEMPLE AND GOD'S SPIRIT LIVES IN YOU?

1 CORINTHIANS 3:16 (CEB)

There exist heavily financed institutes and movements devoted to the construction of a new Jerusalem Temple (and with it the destruction of the Dome of the Rock and *Al-Aqsa* Mosque). Armed Israeli settlers consistently break into the *Al-Aqsa* campus to pray or perform rituals, while Muslim worshippers are frequently harassed.

Meanwhile, Christian Zionist ranchers in Texas have zealously devoted their lives to raising "the perfect red heifer," for the purification and dedication of a new temple.[1] Christian Zionist tourists flock to the Western Wall, yet hardly acknowledge the existence of the Church of the Holy Sepulcher as the traditional site of Christ's death and resurrection, let alone the "living stones" who are the Indigenous Palestinian worshippers.

The Temple is seen in the Bible as the place where God would "dwell" with his people. As Colin Chapman tells us, "The root word *dwell* in Hebrew is *shakan*, and from it is derived the word Shekinah, which was used later by the Jews as a way of speaking about the glory of God,"[2] of His divine presence.

However, embedded within the biblical narrative, from even the very construction and dedication of the Temple itself, is the notion of the Temple's inadequacy as a true dwelling place for the divine presence of God:

THE BIBLE IS ANTI-ZIONIST #5

A. King Solomon's words (in 2 Chronicles) foreshadow and point forward to the eventual destruction and obsolescence of the Temple.

B. "Heaven is my throne, and Earth is my footstool," the prophet Isaiah tells us, declaring that God chooses to dwell instead among "the humble and penitent." Jesus would refer to these as "the poor in spirit," those "to whom belong the Kingdom of Heaven" (Matthew 5:3). Isaiah then speaks of God sending his people out "to declare His glory among the nations," bringing into the fold new family members from among all peoples as an offering to the Lord (Isaiah 66:19-20).

C. Making this mission his own, the Apostle Paul would proclaim in the heart of Athens that "God does not live in temples made by human hands" (Acts 17). D. Instead, as Paul writes to the Corinthians, "You are God's Temple, and God's Spirit lives within you."

Paul, in Romans 15, would explicitly equate his own work to the global vision of Isaiah 66, "working as a priest of God's gospel so that the offering of the Gentiles can be acceptable and made holy by the Holy Spirit" (v. 16). Ultimately, we are the inheritors of a cosmic mission and citizens of a divine kingdom. As such, supporting the construction of a new temple in Jerusalem is not only pointless but an insult to God's majesty and a betrayal of the *missio dei* ("mission of God").

REFLECT

→ Prayerfully read through the verses one more time. Is there a particular word, phrase, or idea that captures your attention?

→ Is there anything new or surprising that you find in the passage? Do you find anything especially challenging?

→ Are you being called to respond or take action in any way?

PRAY

God of Love, we cry out against theologies that justify violence and oppression. Break the chains of hatred masked as faith, and dismantle ideologies that bless injustice. As you guide the faithful in their efforts to promote peace and dignity, we also ask you to awaken hearts numbed by apathy. Stir in us a holy unrest that refuses to accept oppression as destiny and protect the people of Palestine and Israel from further harm. Holy Spirit, fill us with a love that seeks justice, a faith that demands peace, and a hope that overcomes fear.

Lord, in your mercy, hear our prayer.

EXPLORE

Whose Holy City? Jerusalem and the Future of Peace in the Middle East, by Colin Chapman

THE BIBLE IS ANTI-ZIONIST

#6
WHAT ZIONISM DOES

THE BIBLE IS ANTI-ZIONIST #6

DOOM TO THOSE WHO ACQUIRE HOUSE AFTER HOUSE, WHO ANNEX FIELD TO FIELD UNTIL THERE IS NO MORE SPACE LEFT AND ONLY YOU LIVE ALONE IN THE LAND . . .

DOOM TO THOSE WHO DRAG GUILT ALONG WITH CORDS OF FRAUD . . . WHO SAY, " GOD SHOULD HURRY AND WORK FASTER SO WE CAN SEE; LET THE PLAN OF ISRAEL' S HOLY ONE COME QUICKLY, SO WE CAN UNDERSTAND IT.

DOOM TO THOSE WHO CALL EVIL GOOD AND GOOD EVIL, WHO PRESENT DARKNESS AS LIGHT AND LIGHT AS DARKNESS, WHO MAKE BITTERNESS SWEET AND SWEETNESS BITTER . . .

DOOM TO THE WINE-SWIGGING WARRIORS . . . WHO SPARE THE GUILTY FOR BRIBES, AND ROB THE INNOCENT OF THEIR RIGHTS . . . FOR THEY HAVE REJECTED THE TEACHING OF THE LORD OF HEAVENLY FORCES, AND HAVE DESPISED THE WORD OF ISRAEL' S HOLY ONE.

ISAIAH 5:8,18-24 (CEB)

"Zionism," a fraught term, can encompass multiple definitions and inspire fierce debate, not just between Zionists and anti-Zionists, but among various camps within Zionism itself.

However, like any movement or ideology, Zionism must be evaluated on the basis of its real-world fruit. So, as Palestinian pastor and theologian Munther Isaac tells us, "Zionism is what Zionism does!"[1]

In Isaiah 5:8, the prophet condemns the unjust acquisition of homes and land:

- Since 1967, Israeli settlers have seized nearly 500,000 acres of Palestinian land in the West Bank.
- In the 1948 *Nakba* (the ethnic cleansing of historic Palestine), Zionist forces destroyed an estimated 52,000 Palestinian homes.
- Since 1967, Israel has demolished an estimated 59,367 West Bank homes.
- In Gaza, ~92% of all housing units have been damaged or destroyed, displacing almost all 2.1 million residents. Demolitions are still underway, as Israelis and American developers plan for settlements.[2]

Verse 18 *condemns those who "traffic in falsehoods and distort reality"*: the Israeli propaganda, or *hasbara*, budget for 2026 is over $725 million, with a significant amount allocated for influence campaigns directly targeting Christian churches, universities, and other religious institutions in the US.[3]

Verse 19 *condemns those preoccupied with hastening the "Day of Judgement"*: there's little need to describe the proliferation and influence of "end-times" preachers and profiteers.

Verse 20 *condemns those who manipulate morality and muddy the waters of right and wrong*: Zionism and Christian Zionism have twisted Jewish and Christian ethical teachings beyond all recognition, to such a point that genocidal evil is declared good.

Verse 22 *condemns the corruption of those tasked with upholding justice, "sparing the guilty for bribes and robbing the innocent of their rights"*: Palestinians live under a draconian apartheid regime. Meanwhile, we are currently witnessing the death of international law in Gaza.

As encountered within "the laboratory of history,"[4] the fruit of Zionism is extraordinarily destructive.

REFLECT

→ Prayerfully read through the verses one more time. Is there a particular word, phrase, or idea that captures your attention?

→ Is there anything new or surprising that you find in the passage? Do you find anything especially challenging?

→ Are you being called to respond or take action in any way?

PRAY

God of Justice and Peace, we lift up the people of all villages under attack crying out for your protection over their homes, holy places, and livelihoods. We lament the hypocrisy of words without action, and the impunity that allows violence to flourish. Strengthen the hearts of those who endure these assaults, and stir the conscience of leaders to move beyond statements to true justice. May your light shine in the darkness, bringing an end to terror, and may your Spirit sustain all who long for peace, dignity, and safety.

Lord, in your mercy, hear our prayer.

EXPLORE

The Other Side of the Wall: A Palestinian Christian Narrative of Lament and Hope, by Munther Isaac

THE BIBLE IS ANTI-ZIONIST

#7

REEDS & BRANCHES

THE BIBLE IS ANTI-ZIONIST #7

WHAT SORROW FOR THOSE WHO SAY THAT EVIL IS GOOD AND GOOD IS EVIL, THAT DARK IS LIGHT AND LIGHT IS DARK, THAT BITTER IS SWEET AND SWEET IS BITTER . . .

ISAIAH 5:20 (NLT)

IN A SINGLE DAY THE LORD WILL DESTROY BOTH THE HEAD AND THE TAIL, THE NOBLE PALM BRANCH AND THE LOWLY REED. THE LEADERS OF ISRAEL ARE THE HEAD, AND THE LYING PROPHETS ARE THE TAIL. FOR THE LEADERS OF THE PEOPLE HAVE MISLED THEM.

ISAIAH 9:14-15 (NLT)

WHAT SORROW AWAITS THE UNJUST JUDGES AND THOSE WHO ISSUE UNFAIR LAWS. THEY DEPRIVE THE POOR OF JUSTICE AND DENY THE RIGHTS OF THE NEEDY AMONG MY PEOPLE. THEY PREY ON WIDOWS AND TAKE ADVANTAGE OF ORPHANS.

ISAIAH 10:1-2 (NLT)

Precisely because "Zionism is what Zionism does," the following definition from Jewish Voice for Peace (JVP) is both illuminating and instructive.

According to JVP, "Zionism, in the words of its founders, is an explicitly 'colonial' ideology. Zionism is a 19th century political ideology that claimed Jewish safety required a Jewish-only nation-state . . . as a response to centuries of antisemitic persecution against Jews across Europe. In 1948, Zionist militias established a Jewish state on Palestinian land, instituted a military occupation over Palestinians, and mandated a system of Jewish legal supremacy—apartheid. For 75 years, Zionism has been used to justify massacres of Palestinians by the Israeli military, the destruction of villages and olive groves, and a military occupation that separates families with checkpoints and walls."[1]

Meanwhile, Rev. Dr. Mitri Raheb defines Christian Zionism "as a Christian lobby that supports the Jewish settler colonialism of Palestinian land by using biblical/theological" formulations. "Those who espouse it," Raheb continues, "do not see themselves as engaged in pure political lobbying, but rather as agents of a grand plan from which they read and interpret both scripture and history." This holds true for Christian Zionists on both "liberal" and "conservative" sides of the theological spectrum.[2]

On the other hand, JVP explains, "Being an anti-Zionist means opposing the political ideology of Zionism, which resulted in the expulsion of 750,000 Indigenous Palestinians from their land and homes. It means standing against the creation of a nation-state with exclusive rights for Jews above others on the land.

"Anti-Zionism supports liberation and justice for the Palestinian people, including their right to return to their homes and land. Anti-Zionists believe in a future where all people on the land live in freedom, safety and equality. Zionism suggests Jews require a supremacist nation state to answer the real question of Jewish safety.

"We believe that everywhere in the world, Jews belong and should be safe. Real safety does not grow from guns, checkpoints, walls and a police state. True safety is built through forging real solidarity with all those fighting for a more liberated world."[3]

Truly, it is hard not to conclude that Zionism represents everything the prophets stood against: a wholesale rejection of covenant justice.

REFLECT

→ Prayerfully read through the verses one more time. Is there a particular word, phrase, or idea that captures your attention?

→ Is there anything new or surprising that you find in the passage? Do you find anything especially challenging?

→ Are you being called to respond or take action in any way?

PRAY

God of the Uprooted, we cry out for those facing the threat of erasure. Strengthen the community to resist despair, and strengthen all of us to resist the systems that make dispossession a policy. Let your justice take root in the soil of the land and in the hearts of those who refuse to look away.

Lord, in your mercy, hear our prayer.

EXPLORE

Solidarity Is the Political Version of Love: Lessons from Jewish Anti-Zionist Organizing, by Rabbi Alissa Wise and Rebecca Vilkomerson

THE BIBLE IS ANTI-ZIONIST

#8
BLESSINGS & CURSES

THE BIBLE IS ANTI-ZIONIST #8

THE LORD HAD SAID TO ABRAM, " LEAVE YOUR NATIVE COUNTRY, YOUR RELATIVES, AND YOUR FATHER' S FAMILY, AND GO TO THE LAND THAT I WILL SHOW YOU. I WILL MAKE YOU INTO A GREAT NATION. I WILL BLESS YOU AND MAKE YOU FAMOUS, AND YOU WILL BE A BLESSING TO OTHERS.

I WILL BLESS THOSE WHO BLESS YOU AND CURSE THOSE WHO TREAT YOU WITH CONTEMPT. ALL THE FAMILIES ON EARTH WILL BE BLESSED THROUGH YOU."

GENESIS 12:1-3 (NLT)

" BECAUSE YOU HAVE DONE THIS THING AND HAVE NOT WITHHELD YOUR SON, YOUR ONLY SON, INDEED I WILL GREATLY BLESS YOU, AND I WILL GREATLY MULTIPLY YOUR SEED AS THE STARS OF THE HEAVENS AND AS THE SAND, WHICH IS ON THE SEASHORE; AND YOUR SEED SHALL POSSESS THE GATE OF HIS ENEMIES. AND IN YOUR SEED ALL THE NATIONS OF THE EARTH SHALL BE BLESSED, BECAUSE YOU HAVE OBEYED MY VOICE."

GENESIS 22:16-18 (NASB)

From preachers to pundits and politicians, perhaps no other verse is wielded in defense of the Zionist project as much as Genesis 12:3: "I will bless those who bless you, and I will curse those who curse you."

To receive the blessings of God, the logic goes, one must shower the state of Israel with financial, diplomatic, political, and military support. In the recent words of a US congressperson, failing this is to risk being "cursed by God." Such a reading is beyond problematic, and it's not just because it represents a particularly vacuous and transactional form of prosperity gospel thinking.

To start, Genesis 12 records a direct promise to Abram. It has nothing to do with the modern state of Israel. According to Rev. Dr. Donald Wagner, "Genesis 12:3 states that God initiates a covenant with Abraham, and it is an assumption Israel is included, but this is not the case. There are four uses of Israel in the Bible, and none of them imply or mean a modern state."[1]

As Dr. Gary Burge tells us, "This is a promise for Abraham's immediate context with Egypt."[2]

Furthermore, such interpretations are distinctly modern inventions, tracing their origin to works like Ernest Scofield's 1909 Reference Bible. This work includes Scofield's fanciful notes and commentary within the very pages of Scripture, elevated almost to the point of sacred text themselves.

Notable, however, is the second half of Genesis 12:3: "All the families on earth will be blessed through you." From its inception, the covenant has always been universal in scope, reflecting the love of the one God for the whole of creation.

Weaponizing this passage to limit the covenant, exclude those you dislike, lay claim to another's land, and offer idolatrous, cult-like devotion to a modern nation state misses the point entirely and is profoundly destructive.

REFLECT

→ Prayerfully read through the verses one more time. Is there a particular word, phrase, or idea that captures your attention?

→ Is there anything new or surprising that you find in the passage? Do you find anything especially challenging?

→ Are you being called to respond or take action in any way?

PRAY

Holy God, we grieve the continued acts of erasure by empire, whose deepening disregard for Palestinian identity and dignity only remind us that justice will never come from those in power. In the face of empire, help us to remain steadfast in your promise of liberation. Strengthen those who continue to speak truth from the margins, and awaken the world to answer the call for justice.

Lord, in your mercy, hear our prayer.

EXPLORE

Zionism and the Quest for Justice in the Holy Land, edited by Donald E. Wagner

THE BIBLE IS ANTI-ZIONIST

#9
CHILDREN OF ABRAHAM

THE BIBLE IS ANTI-ZIONIST #9

GOD GAVE THE PROMISES TO ABRAHAM AND HIS CHILD. AND NOTICE THAT THE SCRIPTURE DOESN'T SAY "TO HIS CHILDREN," AS IF IT MEANT MANY DESCENDANTS. RATHER, IT SAYS "TO HIS CHILD"—AND THAT, OF COURSE, MEANS CHRIST . . .

FOR YOU ARE ALL CHILDREN OF GOD THROUGH FAITH IN CHRIST JESUS. AND ALL WHO HAVE BEEN UNITED WITH CHRIST IN BAPTISM HAVE PUT ON CHRIST, LIKE PUTTING ON NEW CLOTHES. THERE IS NO LONGER JEW OR GENTILE, SLAVE OR FREE, MALE AND FEMALE. FOR YOU ARE ALL ONE IN CHRIST JESUS. AND NOW THAT YOU BELONG TO CHRIST,

YOU ARE THE TRUE CHILDREN OF ABRAHAM. YOU ARE HIS HEIRS, AND GOD'S PROMISE TO ABRAHAM BELONGS TO YOU.

GALATIANS 3:16,26-29 (NLT)

THE BIBLE IS ANTI-ZIONIST #9

Following up from last time, nothing in Genesis 12 indicates that blessings and curses must be applied unconditionally or in perpetuity to Abraham's physical decedents, let alone a modern nation state.

But, as Dr. Gary Burge informs us, "Because some people think the promises and blessings follow ethnic lines, then you must have the Jewish ethnicity to benefit from them. It is an ethnic argument. However, the Old Testament prophets and especially the New Testament reject this narrow understanding of identity."[1]

In Galatians 3, the Apostle Paul makes this abundantly clear: "There is no longer Jew or Gentile, slave or free, male and female. For you are all one in Christ Jesus." While honoring diversity is paramount, there is no room for ethnic exclusivity or sectarian supremacy among those who would be the people of God.

Both Zionists and Christian Zionists, however, insert an agenda of exclusivity and ethnic supremacy within the plan of God.

Zionists sanctify settler-colonial conquest and ordain the ethnic cleansing of Palestine.

Referencing the Scofield Reference Bible of Christian Zionism, Burge explains, "It was a dispensational project that believed in the ethnic exclusivity of the Jews in the program of God, and these things were inserted into its footnotes."[2] Scofield's novel interpretations would spread rapidly in the North American context.

As a Christian, however, it is quite natural to take seriously and listen to the words of the New Testament authors, to observe how they read, understand, and apply Old Testament texts.

The Apostle Paul is adamant that the covenant promises of Genesis belong to all on the basis of grace through faith, not race or ethnic identity. Recalling the universal vision at the heart of the Abrahamic covenant, all are invited to be counted as children of Abraham and heirs to whom belong the promises of God.

REFLECT

→ Prayerfully read through the verses one more time. Is there a particular word, phrase, or idea that captures your attention?

→ Is there anything new or surprising that you find in the passage? Do you find anything especially challenging?

→ Are you being called to respond or take action in any way?

PRAY

Holy God, we lift up our beloved siblings from across the world who suffer through horrors hidden and unhidden. We grieve the deep racism and colonialism of a world that deems some lives invisible and disposable, and we confess our own complicity in participating in systems that contribute to their oppression. Holy Spirit, help us understand that all our freedoms are intertwined. In doing so, may we pursue liberation in ways that uplift the voices of all oppressed peoples.

Lord, in your mercy, hear our prayer.

EXPLORE

Whose Land? Whose Promise? What Christians Are Not Being Told About Israel and the Palestinians, by Gary M. Burge

THE BIBLE IS ANTI-ZIONIST

#10

WALLS WILL FALL

IN THOSE DAYS YOU WERE LIVING APART FROM CHRIST. YOU WERE EXCLUDED FROM CITIZENSHIP AMONG THE PEOPLE OF ISRAEL, AND YOU DID NOT KNOW THE COVENANT PROMISES GOD HAD MADE TO THEM. YOU LIVED IN THIS WORLD WITHOUT GOD AND WITHOUT HOPE.

BUT NOW YOU HAVE BEEN UNITED WITH CHRIST JESUS. ONCE YOU WERE FAR AWAY FROM GOD, BUT NOW YOU HAVE BEEN BROUGHT NEAR TO HIM THROUGH THE BLOOD OF CHRIST.

FOR CHRIST HIMSELF HAS BROUGHT PEACE TO US.
HE UNITED JEWS AND GENTILES INTO ONE PEOPLE WHEN, IN HIS OWN BODY ON THE CROSS, HE BROKE DOWN THE WALL OF HOSTILITY THAT SEPARATED US.

HE DID THIS BY ENDING THE SYSTEM OF LAW WITH ITS COMMANDMENTS AND REGULATIONS. HE MADE PEACE BETWEEN JEWS AND GENTILES BY CREATING IN HIMSELF ONE NEW PEOPLE FROM THE TWO GROUPS.

EPHESIANS 2:12-15 (NLT)

Admittedly, and quite understandably, discussing the theological and historical relationship between Christianity and Judaism is fraught with difficulty.

From exclusion and demonization to forced assimilation or even fetishization, Christians—often animated by profoundly destructive theologies—have failed, time and again, to love and honor their Jewish neighbors.

Therefore, it is essential to understand reception history, that is how a passage has been interpreted (and abused!) throughout history, as we seek to challenge problematic readings and make amends for historical injustice.

Part of honoring the religious other, however, is to recognize and affirm authentic differences where they exist. Christianity and Judaism, alongside Islam, share incredible common ground, especially if we allow ourselves to unlearn historic prejudices and meet together face to face. (As informed by recent history, too many Christians are still failing to truly love and honor their Muslim neighbors.)

Nevertheless, each remains a distinct religion, often approaching similar challenges or answering similar questions in distinctive ways in line with their own interpretive traditions and subtraditions. As such, it is completely okay for Christians to utilize Christian logic on the basis of Christ-centered readings of Scripture to answer questions in uniquely Christian ways. Jewish and Muslim interpreters will naturally follow their own internal logics as well.

As it happens, the Jewish authors of the New Testament had a lot to say about the people of God. Theirs is an expansive vision of divinely-ordained unity and inclusivity, welcoming and adopting—but not subsuming or assimilating—Gentile believers as siblings and fellow citizens alongside Jews, building upon the universalist streak embedded within the Hebrew texts. In their logic, one group has not replaced another.

So, it is imperative to reject bigoted and supersessionist theologies while also challenging cynical accusations of "replacement theology" that frequently accompany Christian support for Palestinian rights.

REFLECT

→ Prayerfully read through the verses one more time. Is there a particular word, phrase, or idea that captures your attention?

→ Is there anything new or surprising that you find in the passage? Do you find anything especially challenging?

→ Are you being called to respond or take action in any way?

PRAY

Holy God, you created us in your image and bestowed on us a dignity that can never be taken away. We grieve every act of violence that denies this sacred gift. We lift before you all whose lives have been lost, and all who suffer in body, mind, or spirit. Our hearts are also heavy for families enduring collective punishment, knowing such cycles of harm only deepen hatred and despair. Holy Spirit, strengthen us to resist the temptation of overcoming evil with evil. Guide us instead toward the path of mercy, healing, and restorative justice.

Lord, in your mercy, hear our prayer.

EXPLORE

Zion's Christian Soldiers? The Bible, Israel and the Church, by Stephen Sizer
See also: *Safety through Solidarity: A Radical Guide to Fighting Antisemitism*, by Shane Burley and Ben Lorber

THE BIBLE IS ANTI-ZIONIST

#11 THE TEMPLE

THE BIBLE IS ANTI-ZIONIST #11

ON THE CROSS CHRIST DID AWAY WITH OUR HATRED FOR EACH OTHER. HE ALSO MADE PEACE BETWEEN US AND GOD BY UNITING JEWS AND GENTILES IN ONE BODY.

CHRIST CAME AND PREACHED PEACE TO YOU GENTILES, WHO WERE FAR FROM GOD, AND PEACE TO US JEWS, WHO WERE NEAR GOD. AND BECAUSE OF CHRIST, ALL OF US CAN COME TO THE FATHER BY THE SAME SPIRIT.

YOU GENTILES ARE NO LONGER STRANGERS AND FOREIGNERS. YOU ARE CITIZENS WITH EVERYONE ELSE WHO BELONGS TO THE FAMILY OF GOD. YOU ARE LIKE A BUILDING WITH THE APOSTLES AND PROPHETS AS THE FOUNDATION AND WITH CHRIST AS THE MOST IMPORTANT STONE.

CHRIST IS THE ONE WHO HOLDS THE BUILDING TOGETHER AND MAKES IT GROW INTO A HOLY TEMPLE FOR THE LORD. AND YOU ARE PART OF THAT BUILDING CHRIST HAS BUILT AS A PLACE FOR GOD'S OWN SPIRIT TO LIVE.

EPHESIANS 2:16-22 (CEV)

Christianity was never a replacement for Judaism. Neither should it be viewed simply as an offshoot.

Rather, both Christianity and Rabbinic Judaism emerged largely in tandem, as parallel Jewish movements wrestling with the implications of remaining faithful to God in the wake of Roman occupation and the destruction of the Second Temple.

Like the Babylonian Exile, this was a catastrophic moment necessitating a radical reorientation of Jewish faith and practice. Both Rabbinic and Christian Jews combed their sacred texts for resources to help them process and move forward, eventually resulting in the distinct religious systems we know.[1]

As it happens, a defining motif of the Hebrew scriptures is that of Exile, an extended education in living without temple, land, or power.

While themes of a future, messianic ("eschatological") restoration remained, neither—barring the occasional charismatic figure—was seeking to restore the kingdom by force of arms. Most Christians would quickly lose the plot after gaining power during the reign of Roman Emperor Constantine, but for the last 150 years Zionism has truly become a violent "Constantinian synthesis" of its own.

Ultimately, Rabbinic Judaism would center on textual interpretation filtered through the lens of the oral law traditions.[2] For its part, the New Testament offered a radical reinterpretation of temple theology, focusing on the Divine Presence of God on earth—the *shekinah* (i.e., the Holy Spirit)—centered no longer in the now-defunct Jerusalem temple.[3]

First embodied in the person of Jesus, the Spirit now dwells among the collective temple of God's people spreading throughout the world. In light of this, Christian Zionist aspirations—especially that of a restored Jerusalem temple—are truly nonsensical.

REFLECT

→ Prayerfully read through the verses one more time. Is there a particular word, phrase, or idea that captures your attention?

→ Is there anything new or surprising that you find in the passage? Do you find anything especially challenging?

→ Are you being called to respond or take action in any way?

PRAY

God of Love, in dark times, we are reminded that your Spirit is present through the work of your people. Cultivate in us faith as steadfast as the persistent widow so that in our movement for justice, we do not lose hope. Lord, continue working through the Church and people around the world so that your will be done on earth.

Lord, in your mercy, hear our prayer.

EXPLORE

The Bible and Other Faiths: What Does the Lord Require of Us? by Ida Glaser

THE BIBLE IS ANTI-ZIONIST

#12 COUNTLESS CRIMES

THE BIBLE IS ANTI-ZIONIST #12

AMOS 1 (CEV)

1 I WILL PUNISH SYRIA FOR COUNTLESS CRIMES.
6 I WILL PUNISH PHILISTIA FOR COUNTLESS CRIMES.
9 I WILL PUNISH PHOENICIA FOR COUNTLESS CRIMES.
11 I WILL PUNISH EDOM FOR COUNTLESS CRIMES.
13 I WILL PUNISH AMMON FOR COUNTLESS CRIMES.

AMOS 2 (CEV)

1 I WILL PUNISH MOAB FOR COUNTLESS CRIMES.
4 I WILL PUNISH JUDAH FOR COUNTLESS CRIMES, AND I
WON'T CHANGE MY MIND. THEY HAVE REJECTED MY
TEACHINGS AND REFUSED TO OBEY ME. THEY WERE LED
ASTRAY BY THE SAME FALSE GODS THEIR ANCESTORS
WORSHIPED.
6 I WILL PUNISH ISRAEL FOR COUNTLESS CRIMES, AND I
WON'T CHANGE MY MIND. THEY SELL HONEST PEOPLE
FOR MONEY, AND THE NEEDY ARE SOLD FOR THE PRICE
OF SANDALS. THEY SMEAR THE POOR IN THE DIRT AND
PUSH ASIDE THOSE WHO ARE HELPLESS.

A hallmark of nationalist, sectarian, and hyper-patriotic thinking is an inability to engage in self-criticism. If we see ourselves as the "the good guys," those with "God on our side," then our actions are inherently moral, holy even; our violence is virtuous. But, the violence of our enemies—even their very existence—becomes demonic, an "affront to God."

To illustrate, Steven Miller, architect of many violent and repressive policies in the US, recently declared: "To our enemies: You have nothing to give . . . We have beauty. We have light. We have goodness. We have determination. We have vision. We have strength. We built the world that we inhabit . . . and we will defend this world. We will defend goodness. We will defend light. We will defend virtue . . . You cannot threaten us because we are on the side of goodness. We are on the side of God."[1]

For his part, Israel's Netanyahu would proclaim: "We will continue to act together with great force and great determination to protect our countries, and, I may add, to protect our common civilization because we're engaged in the battle of civilization against barbarism."[2]

As to what this looks like in practice, Israeli Finance Minister Bezalel Smotrich recently referred to the forced starvation of two million Palestinians in Gaza as both "just and moral."[3] When taken to its logical end, the result of such dualistic thinking is genocide.

The beauty of the prophetic witness, however, is in God's refusal to play partisan games. Oppression is condemned and God's judgement falls upon friend and foe alike.

The first chapters of Amos are organized in such a way as to highlight this exact point, framing what is ultimately a scathing internal rebuke. Identifying as "the people of God" is in no way an excuse for injustice or "sanctified" violence. Yet, these are the claims of Zionism.

Ultimately, sectarian thinking—including Zionism, Christian Nationalism, American exceptionalism, and racial supremacy (I could apply this to various Islamist movements as well)—is an affront to the monotheistic vision.

REFLECT

→ Prayerfully read through the verses one more time. Is there a particular word, phrase, or idea that captures your attention?

→ Is there anything new or surprising that you find in the passage? Do you find anything especially challenging?

→ Are you being called to respond or take action in any way?

PRAY

Holy God, you hear the cries of the innocent and the groans of a world aching for peace. We grieve the lives lost to the arrogance of empires, who in their greed and thirst for power, continue to unleash violence across the region. O Lord, we echo the Psalmist's plea: scatter the nations that delight in war (Psalm 68:30). Turn the hearts of complicit leaders toward repentance, and let your Spirit move through the rubble, present with all who suffer. We pray for an end to all wars and a just peace to prevail.

Lord, in your mercy, hear our prayer.

EXPLORE

The Bible and the Palestine Israel Conflict, edited by Naim Ateek, Cedar Duaybis, and Tina Whitehead

image[4]

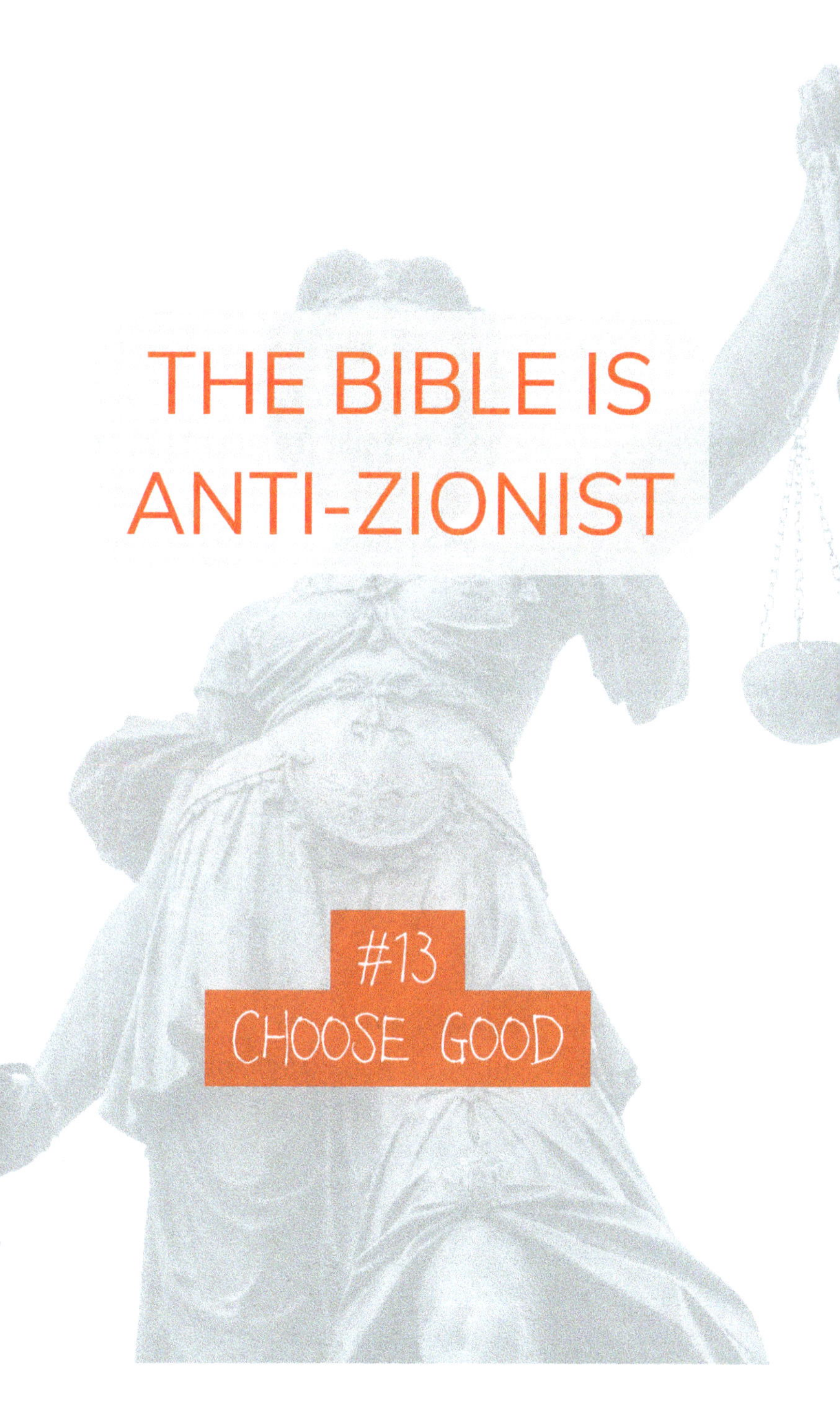
THE BIBLE IS
ANTI-ZIONIST
#13
CHOOSE GOOD

THE BIBLE IS ANTI-ZIONIST #13

YOU PEOPLE HATE JUDGES AND HONEST WITNESSES; YOU ABUSE THE POOR AND DEMAND HEAVY TAXES FROM THEM. YOU HAVE BUILT EXPENSIVE HOMES, BUT YOU WON'T ENJOY THEM; YOU HAVE PLANTED VINEYARDS, BUT YOU WILL GET NO WINE.
I AM THE LORD, AND I KNOW YOUR TERRIBLE SINS. YOU CHEAT HONEST PEOPLE AND TAKE BRIBES; YOU ROB THE POOR OF JUSTICE. TIMES ARE SO EVIL THAT ANYONE WITH GOOD SENSE WILL KEEP QUIET.

IF YOU REALLY WANT TO LIVE, YOU MUST STOP DOING WRONG AND START DOING RIGHT. I, THE LORD GOD ALL-POWERFUL, WILL THEN BE ON YOUR SIDE, JUST AS YOU CLAIM I AM.

CHOOSE GOOD INSTEAD OF EVIL! SEE THAT JUSTICE IS DONE. MAYBE I, THE LORD ALL-POWERFUL, WILL BE KIND TO WHAT'S LEFT OF YOUR PEOPLE

AMOS 5:10-15 (CEV)

God establishes a covenant, first with Abraham and then with the newly created nation, that "it might carry out God's plans for human salvation," and that all peoples on earth might be blessed through it.

There was an expectation of reciprocity. And, this was to be accomplished explicitly "through their ethical behavior."

As Daryl P. Domning writes, "The promises were conditioned on the nation's doing justice," such that "their tenure in the land was conditioned on obedience to this covenant . . . and not idolatry of the promise itself."[1]

As it happens, Zionism is a perfect expression of "idolatry to the promise itself," expecting the land while simultaneously failing to recognize the reciprocal demands for justice expected of those who would claim to be the people of God.

In light of this covenantal context, the prophet Amos excoriates the Israelites for gross infidelity to the covenant. It's an infidelity expressed in the oppression of society's most vulnerable, by means of economic exploitation, the suppression of truth, the denial of justice, and the corruption of those systems intended to uphold justice.

Reading these words of the prophet, I cannot therefore fathom the twisted logic of those Zionist settlers or their Christian Zionist financiers who believe that this settler-colonial enterprise—built from its origins upon bigotry, violence, and theft—can possibly represent the will of God.

As fellow prophet Micah would exclaim, "What sorrow awaits you who lie awake at night, thinking up evil plans. You rise at dawn and hurry to carry them out, simply because you have the power to do so. When you want a piece of land, you find a way to seize it. When you want someone's house, you take it by fraud and violence. You cheat a man of his property, stealing his family's inheritance" (2:1-2).

REFLECT

→ Prayerfully read through the verses one more time. Is there a particular word, phrase, or idea that captures your attention?

→ Is there anything new or surprising that you find in the passage? Do you find anything especially challenging?

→ Are you being called to respond or take action in any way?

PRAY

Holy God, we lament the relentless theft of land and breach of international law. As new settlements rise on stolen soil, we ask you to be present with those who face dispossession and to illuminate to the world the machinery of occupation at work. Tear down the walls of injustice and plant in us the courage to resist every act of erasure. May we stand with the uprooted and labor for a future where all may dwell in safety and freedom.

Lord, in your mercy, hear our prayer.

EXPLORE

Zionism through Christian Lenses: Ecumenical Perspectives on the Promised Land, edited by Carole Monica Burnett

THE BIBLE IS ANTI-ZIONIST

#14
OCEANS OF JUSTICE

THE BIBLE IS ANTI-ZIONIST #14

I CAN'T STAND YOUR RELIGIOUS MEETINGS. I'M FED UP WITH YOUR CONFERENCES AND CONVENTIONS. I WANT NOTHING TO DO WITH YOUR RELIGION PROJECTS, YOUR PRETENTIOUS SLOGANS AND GOALS. I'M SICK OF YOUR FUND-RAISING SCHEMES, YOUR PUBLIC RELATIONS AND IMAGE MAKING. I'VE HAD ALL I CAN TAKE OF YOUR NOISY EGO-MUSIC. WHEN WAS THE LAST TIME YOU SANG TO ME? DO YOU KNOW WHAT I WANT? I WANT JUSTICE—OCEANS OF IT. I WANT FAIRNESS—RIVERS OF IT. THAT'S WHAT I WANT. THAT'S ALL I WANT? (THE MESSAGE).

I HATE, I DESPISE YOUR FEAST DAYS, AND I DO NOT SAVOR YOUR SACRED ASSEMBLIES. THOUGH YOU OFFER ME BURNT OFFERINGS AND YOUR GRAIN OFFERINGS, I WILL NOT ACCEPT THEM, NOR WILL I REGARD YOUR FATTENED PEACE OFFERINGS. TAKE AWAY FROM ME THE NOISE OF YOUR SONGS, FOR I WILL NOT HEAR THE MELODY OF YOUR STRINGED INSTRUMENTS. BUT LET JUSTICE RUN DOWN LIKE WATER, AND RIGHTEOUSNESS LIKE A MIGHTY STREAM (NKVJ).

AMOS 5:21-24

THE BIBLE IS ANTI-ZIONIST #14

I recently came across a social media post by the anti-Zionist group, Jewish Voice for Peace (JVP). It contained a photo of Israeli army soldiers celebrating Rosh Hashanah amid the ruins of the Jenin Palestinian refugee camp.

An excerpt reads, "Rosh Hashanah instructs us to begin the process of turning inwards–*Teshuvah*–reflecting on the ways we have done harm. Israeli soldiers eating a celebratory meal on the rubble of families' homes in a refugee camp that they helped destroy epitomizes the opposite of *Teshuvah*. In this, as in so many ways, Zionism corrodes the spiritual impulse of the holiday."[1]

I am not Jewish, but I have certainly seen my fair share of holidays twisted beyond all recognition. In the way that Christian Nationalism and Christian Zionism make a mockery of New Testament faith, I fully understand how Zionism can be seen as a betrayal of the very Judaism it claims to represent.

Too often, we are guilty in our self-obsessed worship of trying to love God while simultaneously ignoring, or directly causing, the dispossession of our neighbors in need. This, the prophets tell us, is impossible.

In Palestine, religious ideologies and institutions have been employed, time and again, to support violent dispossession and oppression. There exists a multiplicity of Christian Zionist organizations working to provide theological justification, financial capital, and political cover for land confiscation, ethnic cleansing, settlement expansion, apartheid, and now genocide. I can't help but see this as a case of religious faith gone horribly wrong.

In Scripture, the prophets remind us time and again of that which truly matters to God: justice for those most vulnerable and at risk. And yet, we find here another situation in which religious devotion is weaponized to support profound injustice.

REFLECT

→ Prayerfully read through the verses one more time. Is there a particular word, phrase, or idea that captures your attention?

→ Is there anything new or surprising that you find in the passage? Do you find anything especially challenging?

→ Are you being called to respond or take action in any way?

PRAY

We remember that you are the God who hears the cry of the suffering, who walks with the persecuted, and who breaks the chains of fear and injustice. Let justice roll down like a mighty river, and righteousness like an ever-flowing stream. Let hatred, terror, and sectarian violence be cast down, and may the power of Your liberating love rise up through Your people.

Lord, in your mercy, hear our prayer.

EXPLORE

Justice and Only Justice: A Palestinian Theology of Liberation, by Naim Stifan Ateek.
See also: *"Thou Shalt Not Stand Idly By": Jews of Conscience on Palestine*, edited by Susan Landau

THE BIBLE IS
ANTI-ZIONIST
END THE APARTHEID
#15
NO LESS IMPORTANT
evesketches

THE BIBLE IS ANTI-ZIONIST #15

But go over to Calneh and see what happened there. Then go to the great city of Hamath and down to the Philistine city of Gath. You are no better than they were and look at how they were destroyed.

AMOS 6:2 (NLT)

He built his palace in the heavens and let its foundations rest on the earth. He scoops up the ocean and empties it on the earth. His name is the Lord.

Israel, I am the Lord God, and the Ethiopians are no less important to me than you are. I brought you out of Egypt, but I also brought the Philistines from Crete and the Arameans from Kir.

AMOS 9:6-7 (CEV)

The Hebrew scriptures relay the story of God's relationship with a specific people, the ancient Israelites. Yet this story—of a particular family, kingdom(s), and people group—is always embedded within a much broader, universal narrative: God's reconciling and restoration of all humankind and even creation itself.

This, after all, is a natural outgrowth of the monotheistic vision, the recognition that the ONE God is the God of everyone. So, as "a nation of priests and kings" called to be a "light unto the nations," the Israelites were always meant to serve more like an "avatar" (to borrow a term) for all humankind.[1] In Christian thought, this calling was taken up in the person of Jesus and, later, the inclusive and expanded people of God.

Amos 6:2 is a reminder to the Israelites that their chosen status is neither on account of, nor does it afford them, any innate superiority in relation to their Levantine neighbors. "You are no better than the Philistines," God declares, and are susceptible therefore to the very same judgement.

The reality of this comparison, however, runs much deeper than judgement.

While Verse 6 reminds us that God transcends any territorial or earthly boundary, Verse 7 recalls the single most formative event in the history of the ancient Hebrews—their deliverance from slavery in Egypt—and the very foundation of their identity as the people of God.

Yet, in the context of Amos, such a foundational event is equivalent in value to God's bringing "the Philistines from Crete or the Arameans from Kir [Mesopotamia]." It's a reminder that even our most sacred of beliefs must never become a tool for the exclusion, dispossession, or oppression of another.

This declaration in no way lessens the importance of God's particular work among the ancient Israelites or the importance of this work for what theologians refer to as "salvation history."

It does, however, directly challenge key Zionist assumptions as an ideology of divine right and racial privilege.

REFLECT

→ Prayerfully read through the verses one more time. Is there a particular word, phrase, or idea that captures your attention?

→ Is there anything new or surprising that you find in the passage? Do you find anything especially challenging?

→ Are you being called to respond or take action in any way?

PRAY

God, help us to not turn our eyes and hearts from the suffering of our brothers and sisters. We confess our inability to stop this genocide and for the numbness of this world that allows schools to be bombed and families to be forcefully separated. Holy Spirit, bring comfort to the victims of oppression and strengthen our resolve to act in your liberatory love.

Lord, in your mercy, hear our prayer.

EXPLORE

Through My Enemy's Eyes: Envisioning Reconciliation in Israel-Palestine, by Salim Munayer and Lisa Loden

Artist: Eva Carballeira R (@evesketches)

THE BIBLE IS ANTI-ZIONIST

#16
A STRANGE ANTICLIMAX

THE BIBLE IS ANTI-ZIONIST #16

PETER GOT UP AND SAID: "MY FRIENDS, YOU KNOW THAT GOD DECIDED LONG AGO TO LET ME BE THE ONE FROM YOUR GROUP TO PREACH THE GOOD NEWS TO THE GENTILES . . . AND HE SHOWED HE HAD CHOSEN THE GENTILES, WHEN HE GAVE THEM THE HOLY SPIRIT, JUST AS HE HAD GIVEN HIS SPIRIT TO US. GOD TREATED THEM IN THE SAME WAY THAT HE TREATED US. THEY PUT THEIR FAITH IN HIM, AND HE MADE THEIR HEARTS PURE . . ."

AFTER THEY HAD FINISHED SPEAKING, JAMES SAID: "MY FRIENDS, LISTEN TO ME! SIMON PETER HAS TOLD HOW GOD FIRST CAME TO THE GENTILES AND MADE SOME OF THEM HIS OWN PEOPLE. THIS AGREES WITH WHAT THE PROPHETS WROTE:

'I, THE LORD, WILL RETURN AND REBUILD DAVID'S FALLEN HOUSE. I WILL BUILD IT FROM ITS RUIN AND SET IT UP AGAIN. THEN OTHER NATIONS WILL TURN TO ME AND BE MY CHOSEN ONES. I, THE LORD, SAY THIS. I PROMISED IT LONG AGO' [FROM **AMOS 9:11-12**; LXX]."

ACTS 15:7-9,13-18 (CEV)

Amos predicted the destruction of the northern Kingdom of Israel, occurring at the hands of the Assyrians in the year 733. Over 130 years later, a similar fate would befall the southern Kingdom of Judah at the hands of the Babylonians.

Known as the Exile, this destruction constitutes the dominant motif of the Hebrew scriptures, as much of the Bible wrestles with explaining why the Exile happened, how to live faithfully in the midst of exile, and maintaining hope in the promise that exile will indeed come an end.

Of the faithful remnant who would survive the Exile, the prophet declares: "At my command, all of you will be sifted like grain. Israelites who remain faithful will be scattered among the nations," but God also promises to, "rebuild the fallen tent of David" (Amos 9:9).

If we translate the prophet's words in the Greek Old Testament (the Septuagint), the version known to the Apostles and the early church, this happens, "so that the rest of humanity, including the Gentiles—all those I have called to be mine—might seek me" (Amos 9:12 LXX).

In the book of Acts, when confronted with the challenge of Gentile believers—specifically in light of the Holy Spirit's presence among them—the Apostles looked to the words of Amos for guidance.

As Colin Chapman explains, "[James] is trying to show that the inclusion of the gentiles in the church is [the] fulfilment of Amos' prophecy about the restoration of Israel and the nations calling on the name of the Lord.

"He understands this restoration of Israel not as something still in the future, but as something that has already taken place in the coming of Christ . . . The fact that gentiles have received the Holy Spirit is evidence that the restoration of Israel described by Amos has already been completed."[1]

Claiming that such prophecies also point to the postponed establishment of an ethno-territorial, settler-colonial state at some predetermined, yet undisclosed date in the distant future "must seem by comparison," to quote Chapman, "a strange anti-climax."[2]

REFLECT

→ Prayerfully read through the verses one more time. Is there a particular word, phrase, or idea that captures your attention?

→ Is there anything new or surprising that you find in the passage? Do you find anything especially challenging?

→ Are you being called to respond or take action in any way?

PRAY

Sovereign God, you are the peace of the world. Even when the world seems filled with conflict and despair, we trust that you are at work, bringing hope and restoration. We continue to pray for a ceasefire in Gaza and for your justice to come to the whole world. Lord, we long for a day where all theologies of empire are replaced with the theologies of your all-inclusive, everlasting love. Until this day comes, strengthen our faith in your promises and to walk in your ways.

Lord, in your mercy, hear our prayer.

EXPLORE

Christian Zionism and the Restoration of Israel: How Should We Interpret the Scriptures? by Colin Chapman

THE BIBLE IS ANTI-ZIONIST

#17
DECLARED CLEAN

THE BIBLE IS ANTI-ZIONIST #17

PETER FELL INTO A TRANCE. HE SAW THE SKY OPEN, AND SOMETHING LIKE A LARGE SHEET WAS LET DOWN BY ITS FOUR CORNERS. IN THE SHEET WERE ALL SORTS OF ANIMALS, REPTILES, AND BIRDS. THEN A VOICE SAID TO HIM, "GET UP, PETER; KILL AND EAT THEM." — "NO, LORD," PETER DECLARED. "I HAVE NEVER EATEN ANYTHING THAT OUR JEWISH LAWS HAVE DECLARED IMPURE AND UNCLEAN." — BUT THE VOICE SPOKE AGAIN: "DO NOT CALL SOMETHING UNCLEAN IF GOD HAS MADE IT CLEAN" . . .

PETER TOLD THEM, "YOU KNOW IT IS AGAINST OUR LAWS FOR A JEWISH MAN TO ENTER A GENTILE HOME LIKE THIS OR TO ASSOCIATE WITH YOU. BUT GOD HAS SHOWN ME THAT I SHOULD NO LONGER THINK OF ANYONE AS IMPURE OR UNCLEAN . . . I SEE VERY CLEARLY THAT GOD SHOWS NO FAVORITISM. IN EVERY NATION HE ACCEPTS THOSE WHO FEAR HIM AND DO WHAT IS RIGHT . . ."

EVEN AS PETER WAS SAYING THESE THINGS, THE HOLY SPIRIT FELL UPON ALL WHO WERE LISTENING TO THE MESSAGE.

ACTS 10:9-15,28,34,44 (NLT)

Palestinian theologian Anton Deik relays the story of a high-profile evangelist posing the following question to a collection of Christian leaders, "Why is the number of people coming to Christ significantly less in Palestine than in other Arab countries?"

According to Deik, "The answer came back sharp and clear from a Muslim-background believer: Christian Zionism."[1] This topic may be uncomfortable for some, but there is an important point needing to be made: *so enmeshed is Christian Zionism within evangelical witness that, when it comes to Palestine, most evangelicals stop being evangelical!*

As Deik explains, this "intertwining of evangelism and Christian Zionism is a major stumbling block to the Gospel."[2]

1. Christian Zionism "portrays God as a god of favoritism, one who prefers the Jews and discriminates against the Arabs on the basis of bloodline."

2. The Bible "is used 'to threaten our existence as Christian and Muslim Palestinians.'"

3. Instead of the good news—the *evangel*, or Gospel—of Christ, "Christian Zionism brings news of discrimination, war and death."[3]

Truly, Christians Zionism is a total inversion of the mission and message of Jesus.

"In the first nine chapters of the book of Acts we do not see the Gospel reaching the Gentiles," Deik explains. "The early church in first-century Palestine grappled with something comparable to Christian Zionism. As Jewish believers, early Christians were impacted by the strong nationalist theology of Second Temple Judaism. Like other Jewish sects of their time . . . they believed that God treated them differently than other nations."[4] In Acts 10, however, we witness the final "conversion" of Peter.

Ultimately, "Before the church could preach the gospel to the world, God had to cleanse his church from its false theology: how it looked at the other and the way it understood God. Only then was the church able to preach the Gospel to the nations."[5]

REFLECT

→ Prayerfully read through the verses one more time. Is there a particular word, phrase, or idea that captures your attention?

→ Is there anything new or surprising that you find in the passage? Do you find anything especially challenging?

→ Are you being called to respond or take action in any way?

PRAY

God of Solidarity, we thank you for the voices that speak out against oppression and stand in unity with those who suffer. Bless these leaders and all who work to bridge divides with courage and empathy. May their witness inspire change and lead to a future where liberation belongs to all. Holy Spirit, we ask you to continue protecting all communities and to lead our hearts and minds so we can serve where we are most needed.

Lord, in your mercy, hear our prayer.

EXPLORE

More Desired than Our Owne Salvation: The Roots of Christian Zionism, by Robert O. Smith
See also: *Being Christian After the Desolation of Gaza*, edited by Bruce Fisk and Ross Wagner

THE BIBLE IS ANTI-ZIONIST

#18

STARING AT CLOUDS

THE BIBLE IS ANTI-ZIONIST #18

JESUS APPEARED TO [THE DISCIPLES] OVER A PERIOD OF FORTY DAYS AND SPOKE ABOUT THE KINGDOM OF GOD . . .

THEN THEY GATHERED AROUND HIM AND ASKED HIM, "LORD, ARE YOU AT THIS TIME GOING TO RESTORE THE KINGDOM TO ISRAEL?"

HE SAID TO THEM: "IT IS NOT FOR YOU TO KNOW THE TIMES OR DATES THE FATHER HAS SET BY HIS OWN AUTHORITY. BUT YOU WILL RECEIVE POWER WHEN THE HOLY SPIRIT COMES ON YOU; AND YOU WILL BE MY WITNESSES IN JERUSALEM, AND IN ALL JUDEA AND SAMARIA, **AND TO THE ENDS OF THE EARTH."**

AFTER HE SAID THIS, HE WAS TAKEN UP BEFORE THEIR VERY EYES, AND A CLOUD HID HIM FROM THEIR SIGHT. THEY WERE LOOKING INTENTLY UP INTO THE SKY AS HE WAS GOING, WHEN SUDDENLY TWO MEN DRESSED IN WHITE STOOD BESIDE THEM. "MEN OF GALILEE," THEY SAID, "WHY DO YOU STAND HERE LOOKING INTO THE SKY?"

ACTS 1:3,6-11 (NIV)

Pulpits, podcasts, publishing houses (and even political offices!) are overflowing with so-called "prophecy watchers," individuals and organizations so obsessed with "The End Times" that it has become the central defining feature of their socio-religious worldview and identity. Very often, the modern State of Israel, coupled with a highly ideological (and frankly racist!) reading of current events, occupies a central position within this worldview.

Yet, like the angels to the disciples, I can't help but question: "Why do you stand here looking into the sky?!" Stop it. You have much more important work to do as ambassadors of the much greater and more expansive Reign of God! The disciples had to be divested of their narrow "Zionist" thinking.

Scholars posit that the Book of Acts was written as a counterpart to the Book of Joshua.[1] Whereas Joshua depicts a process of violent conquest, Acts details the growth and expansion of the Reign of God to the ends of the known world—a nonviolent process of "grassroots" social transformation that Jesus likens to yeast quietly working its way through dough (Matthew 13:33).

Rather than conquest, the Apostle Paul describes the *kerygma*, the gospel "proclamation" of Christ's lordship as the means by which believers lay claim to their inheritance. He would later declare, "And now I entrust you to God and the message of his grace that is able to build you up and give you an inheritance with all those he has set apart for himself" (Acts 20:32).

"Mission to the world," NT Wright tells us, "seems to have taken the place held, within the Jewish symbolic universe, by the land."[2] As Jesus explains, "The holy nation of heaven is like mustard seed." It is an inversion of earthly power, the way of the cross.

Moreover, in New Testament thinking, the Temple was now viewed as obsolete. The curtain to the Holy of Holies had torn wide open at the death of Jesus, serving no longer as the earthly home of the Holy Spirit. Instead, the Divine Presence would dwell ("tabernacle") amongst the collective assembly of believers, as they spread throughout the world. Now, the "holy land" is understood as being comprised of the entire world and its diversity of peoples.

The Kingdom of Israel has ceded power to the cosmic Reign of God. Therefore, to be a Christian Zionist is to rewind the clock of salvation history—remaining stuck in the past even as they keep trying to predict the future.

REFLECT

→ Prayerfully read through the verses one more time. Is there a particular word, phrase, or idea that captures your attention?

→ Is there anything new or surprising that you find in the passage? Do you find anything especially challenging?

→ Are you being called to respond or take action in any way?

PRAY

Incarnate Christ, we give thanks for the prophetic voices rising across the world. Lord, continue to guide the Church to sow seeds of revolutionary love, speaking truth boldly and standing with the oppressed. We pray that all church leaders will remain faithful to Christ as they continue to work for justice, peace, and reconciliation.

Lord, in your mercy, hear our prayer.

EXPLORE

Whose Promised Land? The Continuing Conflict over Israel and Palestine, by Colin Chapman

THE BIBLE IS ANTI-ZIONIST

#19 DISPOSSESSION

THE BIBLE IS ANTI-ZIONIST #19

Now there was a man named Naboth, from Jezreel, who owned a vineyard in Jezreel beside the palace of King Ahab of Samaria. One day Ahab said to Naboth, "Since your vineyard is so convenient to my palace, I would like to buy it to use as a vegetable garden. I will give you a better vineyard in exchange, or if you prefer, I will pay you for it." – But Naboth replied, "The Lord forbid that I should give you the inheritance that was passed down by my ancestors."

The elders and other town leaders followed the instructions Jezebel had written in the letters. They called for a fast and put Naboth at a prominent place before the people. Then the two scoundrels came and sat down across from him. And they accused Naboth before all the people, saying, "He cursed God and the king." So he was dragged outside the town and stoned to death. The town leaders then sent word to Jezebel, "Naboth has been stoned to death."

1 Kings 21:1-3,11-14 (NLT)

In my reading, I am immediately struck by the royal family's corrupt manipulation of religious sentiment to whip up popular opinion against Naboth, legitimizing his murder for the sake of expropriating the land and extracting its natural resources.

Unfortunately, I can't help thinking about present-day realities: at the time of writing, my country just invaded Venezuela in order to remove its president from power and open up the land for exploitation by American oil companies. Sadly, this is only the latest in a long line of similar interventions both in and beyond Latin America. I also wish to acknowledge that I am currently writing from the traditional, unceded lands of the Indigenous Ohlone people, a society greatly harmed by Spanish and U.S. settlement.

Naturally, the Iraq War also comes to mind. But, the script is old. I can't help but recall the CIA and MI6 engineered coup of 1953 in response to the nationalization of Iranian oil (the fallout of which we are feeling to the present day). The script can be traced back to the initial British conquest of Egypt and French colonization of Algeria in the 19th century, but it is as old as time.[1]

However, I am especially reminded of Israel's planned expropriation of natural gas reserves in the Palestinian waters off Gaza; the exploration licenses have already been granted.[2]

From my own socio-cultural vantage point, King Ahab's offer to purchase Naboth's vineyard looks entirely reasonable. Naboth's refusal is counterintuitive. At issue, however, is not a land dispute gone horribly awry but two contradictory conceptions of property and possession.

"For Naboth," Walter Brueggemann explains, "his property is an 'inheritance'; for Ahab, the same property is a 'possession' without familial, historical, or sentimental linkage. From his perspective, Naboth has no option but to refuse the offer of the king."[3] Additionally, Brueggemann writes, "Naboth . . . belonged to his land as much as his land belonged to him. He identifies his vineyard as 'my ancestral home.'"[4]

Much has been written about the contrast between Indigenous versus settler-colonial conceptions of land and property, very much mirroring the different stances of Ahab and Naboth. By definition, settler colonialism works to conquer, cleanse, colonize, and then exploit the land, as a possession; meanwhile, Indigenous societies frequently speak of their relationship to the land in terms of identity, spirituality, family, culture, and belonging.

REFLECT

→ Prayerfully read through the verses one more time. Is there a particular word, phrase, or idea that captures your attention?

→ Is there anything new or surprising that you find in the passage? Do you find anything especially challenging?

→ Are you being called to respond or take action in any way?

PRAY

Good God, we come before you grieving this news. We remember that "in arrogance the wicked persecute the poor— let them be caught in the schemes they have devised" (Psalm 10:1-2). In the face of injustice, we declare you are a just and righteous God who sees all evil deeds and will deliver us from our oppression. As we pray to you in lament, we ask you to be with the displaced and suffering. Help us to be better witnesses to the injustices occurring in the West Bank.

Lord in your mercy, hear our prayer.

EXPLORE

Faith in the Face of Empire: The Bible through Palestinian Eyes, by Mitri Raheb
See also: "Noticing Sumac in Unexpected Places," by Shadia Qubti in *The Cross and the Olive Tree: Cultivating Palestinian Theology amid Gaza*

THE BIBLE IS
ANTI-ZIONIST
#20
SUMUD

THE BIBLE IS ANTI-ZIONIST #20

When Jezebel heard the news, she said to Ahab, "You know the vineyard Naboth wouldn't sell you? Well, you can have it now! He's dead!" So Ahab immediately went down to the vineyard of Naboth to claim it.

But the Lord said to Elijah, "Go down to meet King Ahab of Israel, who rules in Samaria. He will be at Naboth's vineyard in Jezreel, claiming it for himself. Give him this message: 'This is what the Lord says: Wasn't it enough that you killed Naboth? Must you rob him, too? Because you have done this, dogs will lick your blood at the very place where they licked the blood of Naboth!'"

"So, my enemy, you have found me!" Ahab exclaimed to Elijah.

"Yes," Elijah answered, "I have come because you have sold yourself to what is evil in the Lord's sight . . . for you have made me very angry and have led Israel into sin.'

1 Kings 21:15-21 (NLT)

As expressed by renowned Palestinian poet Mahmoud Darwish, "The land we carry in our blood."[1]

Indigenous Palestinians speak often of their deep rootedness to the land, expressed symbolically in the image of the iconic Palestinian olive tree. Embedded within extended family, community, and confessional networks, individuals and families have lived on and worked the land together for centuries, millennia even.

I recently came across the following words on a popular Palestinian advocacy website, "For Palestinians, the land has a meaning that extends beyond borders, nationality or property. The relationship between Palestinians and their land is rooted in thousands of years of existence, labor and culture. The country is not a backdrop to their history — it is their history."[2]

Central to Palestinian identity, the manner in which this rootedness is spoken about frequently takes on spiritual overtones, and it has long given shape to Palestinian resistance: in the form of sumud, or the steadfast refusal to give up or give in.

Likewise, from the advent of Zionist colonization in the late 19th century to the present day, Palestinian refugees speak of an extreme sense of loss and alienation at being violently uprooted from their lands and homes, their native soil.

"In every olive tree, in every citrus fruit, in every stone of a village wall," the unnamed writer cited above continues, "lives a story of steadfastness and return. Despite decades of colonization, occupation and uprooting, Palestinians remain rooted in their land. Not out of naivety, but out of conviction: staying is an act of resistance."[3]

Truly, it is impossible to understand the crisis in the Holy Land without understanding the profound historic connection between the Palestinian people and the land.

Knowing this, Israeli settlers and the military frequently target olive groves for destruction, such that an estimated 800,000 plus trees have been uprooted and destroyed since 1967. It is an intentional attack on "identity, memory and future" as much as it is upon the livelihood and economic survival of the Palestinian people, "an attempt to tear the roots of a people away from its history."[4]

REFLECT

→ Prayerfully read through the verses one more time. Is there a particular word, phrase, or idea that captures your attention?

→ Is there anything new or surprising that you find in the passage? Do you find anything especially challenging?

→ Are you being called to respond or take action in any way?

PRAY

God of the marginalized, we grieve the complicity of the Western church that remains more fixated on policing prophetic voices than stopping the violence of empire. Help us to challenge the silence of our churches by increasing our solidarity and our voices for the oppressed. We pray for true repentance from world leaders and renewed commitment to justice and peace in the Holy Land.

Lord in your mercy, hear our prayer.

EXPLORE

Palestine Is Our Home: Voices of Loss, Courage, and Steadfastness, edited by Nahida Gordon Halaby

THE BIBLE IS ANTI-ZIONIST

#21

PEACE. JOY. LIBERATION.

THE BIBLE IS ANTI-ZIONIST #21

THOSE WHO WALKED IN THE DARK HAVE SEEN A BRIGHT LIGHT. AND IT SHINES UPON EVERYONE WHO LIVES IN THE LAND OF DARKEST SHADOWS.

OUR LORD, YOU HAVE MULTIPLIED YOUR NATION. BECAUSE OF YOU, ITS PEOPLE ARE GLAD AND CELEBRATE LIKE WORKERS AT HARVEST TIME OR LIKE SOLDIERS DIVIDING UP THE PLUNDER [JOY]

YOU HAVE BROKEN THE POWER OF THOSE WHO ABUSED AND ENSLAVED YOUR PEOPLE. YOU HAVE RESCUED THEM JUST AS YOU SAVED YOUR PEOPLE FROM MIDIAN [JUSTICE & LIBERATION]

THE BOOTS OF MARCHING WARRIORS AND THE BLOOD STAINED UNIFORMS HAVE BEEN FED TO FLAMES AND EATEN BY FIRE [PEACE].

A CHILD HAS BEEN BORN FOR US. WE HAVE BEEN GIVEN A SON WHO WILL BE OUR RULER. HIS NAMES WILL BE WONDERFUL ADVISOR AND MIGHTY GOD, ETERNAL FATHER AND PRINCE OF PEACE. HIS POWER WILL NEVER END; PEACE WILL LAST FOREVER. HE WILL RULE DAVID'S KINGDOM AND MAKE IT GROW STRONG. HE WILL ALWAYS RULE WITH HONESTY AND JUSTICE.

ISAIAH 9:2-7 (CEV)

"The main message of the gospel," in the words of John and Samuel Munayer, "is the liberation of all people from all captivity—physical and spiritual—and the inauguration of the Kingdom of God."[1]

For this reason, as recorded in Matthew 4, Jesus inaugurates his public ministry with the above words from the prophet Isaiah, who envisions the inbreaking light of the messianic reign to a world of darkness and injustice.

Each year, this is the hope longed for during Advent (marking the new liturgical year), and it is the hope we carry with us from each moment to the next: both a longing for and a celebration of the JOY, JUSTICE, and PEACE of Christ's liberating reign as the fulfillment of prophetic promise.

The good news, according to Rev. Alex Awad, "is that the stories recorded in the Gospels . . . are stories of hope for the hopeless. Their message is clear: God comes to save, rescue, and redeem his people. He comes to collide with the powers of political, military, and economic structures that oppress the poor to bring them freedom and peace."[2]

"It is also clear," Awad continues, "that God uses ordinary men and women, whom he anoints, and sends them out to do his work of salvation, rescue, and liberation."[3]

This pursuit of kingdom justice, peace, and joy, "on earth as it is in heaven," becomes therefore our mission as followers of Jesus. Needless to say, this hasn't always been the main priority of Christians or Christian institutions.

The greatest obstacles to justice in Palestine are the result of American political calculus and imperial interests. Even so, there are many Christians in the Global South who take their lead from American missionaries, authors and publishers, media personalities, and seminaries—often with deep pockets. This is especially true when it comes to the rapid global expansion of the charismatic New Apostolic Reformation movement.[4]

Unfortunately, the message conveyed is frequently one of American culture, neoliberal values, prosperity theology, and an unquestioning support for Israel. The social and political consequences of this are being felt more and more on the global stage.

For instance, the one dissenting voice in Israel's genocide trial at the International Court of Justice, despite all available evidence, was recorded defending her vote before a church audience in Ghana: "The Lord is counting on me to stand on the side of Israel!"[5]

There are many signs, however, that people around the world are hungry for robust, contextual theologies of liberation, justice, and peace, in contrast to manipulative, theologically shallow, and scripturally suspect justifications for domination, exclusion, and greed—of which Christian Zionism is a prime example (alongside such ideologies as Christian Nationalism and historical evils like Manifest Destiny and the Doctrine of Discovery).

To exchange the joy, justice, and peace of Christ's liberating reign for false theologies of violent domination, wealth extraction, and ethnic exclusion makes a mockery of Isaiah's messianic hope. It makes a mockery of the God revealed to us in the life and witness of Jesus Christ.

REFLECT

→ Prayerfully read through the verses one more time. Is there a particular word, phrase, or idea that captures your attention?

→ Is there anything new or surprising that you find in the passage? Do you find anything especially challenging?

→ Are you being called to respond or take action in any way?

PRAY

Good God, as we witness the actions of empire, we think of the words of Prophet Isaiah: "Woe to those who make unjust laws, to those who issue oppressive decrees, to deprive the poor of their rights and withhold justice from the oppressed" (Isaiah 10:1-2). We trust that you are a righteous judge who will deliver us from injustice. Embolden the world to do more than words and take real action for liberation.

Lord, in your mercy, hear our prayer.

EXPLORE

Palestinian Memories: The Story of a Palestinian Mother and Her People, by Alex Awad

THE BIBLE IS ANTI-ZIONIST

#22 PATERNALISM

JESUS CALLED THEM TOGETHER AND SAID,

"YOU KNOW THAT THE RULERS IN THIS WORLD LORD IT OVER THEIR PEOPLE, AND OFFICIALS FLAUNT THEIR AUTHORITY OVER THOSE UNDER THEM.

BUT AMONG YOU IT WILL BE DIFFERENT.

WHOEVER WANTS TO BE A LEADER AMONG YOU MUST BE YOUR SERVANT, AND WHOEVER WANTS TO BE FIRST AMONG YOU MUST BECOME YOUR SLAVE.

FOR EVEN THE SON OF MAN CAME NOT TO BE SERVED BUT TO SERVE OTHERS AND TO GIVE HIS LIFE AS A RANSOM FOR MANY."

MATTHEW 20:25-28 (NIV)

A. "Imperial Paternalism"[1] - The tragic history of western imperial intervention in the Middle East is rife with examples of theological and ideological systems which have sought to promote, justify, downplay, and excuse that which in reality has been little more than violent conquest, theft, and exploitation.

These colonial theologies, in the words of Brian McClaren, "explain—historically or theologically—why the colonizers deserve to be in power—sustained in the position of hegemony . . . why the colonized deserve to be dominated—maintained in the subaltern or subservient position . . . provide ethical justification for the phases and functions of colonization [and] camouflage or cosmetically enhance its ugly aspects and preempt attempts to expose them."[2]

From the "civilizing missions" of the 19th century, through the post-war Mandates of the 20th, to the modern American desire to "export freedom by force of arms" in the early 21st century, such justifications have a deep history.

With degrading paternalism, in turns both cynical and sincere, imperial powers have justified their aggression by convincing themselves they are acting for the betterment of the colonized peoples.

When it comes to the destruction of Palestine, this is seen most acutely in the British Mandate of Palestine, which actively worked to dismantle Palestinian political institutions and civil society—encouraging Zionist settlement while attempting to project an image of detached neutrality or benevolent overlordship.

The idea of America as an honest peace broker is equally farcical. Likewise, it's true that in the West Asian context "white feminism," "pinkwashing," and other examples of feigned humanitarian concern have a fairly abysmal record. It has even become a joke that westerners only ever seem to care about such matters when a country is about to be invaded or bombed.

Not only does bad theology kill, but it has justified the subjugation and death of countless individuals.

REFLECT

→ Prayerfully read through the verses one more time. Is there a particular word, phrase, or idea that captures your attention?

→ Is there anything new or surprising that you find in the passage? Do you find anything especially challenging?

→ Are you being called to respond or take action in any way?

PRAY

God of Justice and Compassion, we come before you burdened by the misuse of power and the distortion of truth. As resources are committed to controlling narratives and silencing the cries of the oppressed, we pray for courage to confront lies and amplify the voices of those suffering in Gaza and beyond. Lord, we ask for your wisdom to guide those who seek to expose injustice and advocate for peace. Strengthen their resolve and protect them from harm. As we fight to uplift the truth tellers and confront the lies of empire, deliver us from the temptation of overcoming evil with evil.

Lord, in your mercy, hear our prayer.

EXPLORE

The Cross and the Olive Tree: Cultivating Palestinian Theology amid Gaza, by John and Samuel Munayer

THE BIBLE IS
ANTI-ZIONIST
#23
CRUSADERISM

THE BIBLE IS ANTI-ZIONIST #23

God created humanity in God's own image, in the divine image God created them.

Genesis 1:27 (CEB)

You have heard that it was said, You must love your neighbor and hate your enemy. But I say to you, love your enemies and pray for those who harass you so that you will be acting as children of your Father who is in heaven. He makes the sun rise on both the evil and the good and sends rain on both the righteous and the unrighteous.

If you love only those who love you, what reward do you have? Don't even the tax collectors do the same? And if you greet only your brothers and sisters, what more are you doing? Don't even the Gentiles do the same? Therefore, just as your heavenly Father is complete in showing love to everyone, so also you must be complete.

Matthew 5:43-48 (CEB)

B. "Henotheistic Crusaderism"[1] - Henotheism essentially declares: "My God can beat up your God!" It is the "warrior tribe" theology which pits one's own god against those of its neighbors.

This, Joseph Cumming tells us, "takes us to the belief that we must fight to defend the survival of Christian civilization. If necessary, we must kill the enemies of our civilization before they kill us. We must pray that 'our God gives us victory over their Allah-God.'"[2]

In this way of thinking, one's own tribe, clan, or nation becomes the chosen of God fighting an epic struggle against "the forces of darkness and their sub-human minions."

We see this in the Crusades and in the language of Zionism. We see this in the religiously tinged language of the "War on Terror" and in the deeply problematic phrase "Judeo-Christian civilization," an invented concept frequently wielded against our Muslim neighbors.

Palestinians, as people like any other, have certainly not been immune, but such dehumanizing language has been employed throughout the Gaza Genocide (recall: "human animals").

Speaking of war with Iran, Israeli Prime Minister Netanyahu recently declared (in English), "America is fighting *with* Israel for a common goal: to protect our future, to protect civilization against these barbarians . . . We have to be more powerful than the barbarians, or they will not be merely at the gate. They'll crash our gates and destroy our societies."[3]

This is the theology of "God and country," whereby the one God is reduced to a territorial idol, transforming the refugee into an infiltrator, the immigrant into an invader, and the Indigenous into an outcast. It represents a wholesale rejection of our call to costly discipleship and self-sacrificial love.

We see it given expression in the popular apocalyptic fantasies of end-times preachers. Like a bad movie played out on the international stage, Arabs and Middle Easterners get swooped up into this imaginary apocalyptic drama, becoming "the foot soldiers of evil committed to the destruction of God's elect," however defined.

It is a form of bigotry that literally demonizes our West Asian siblings. Once demonized, genocide comes easy.

REFLECT

→ Prayerfully read through the verses one more time. Is there a particular word, phrase, or idea that captures your attention?

→ Is there anything new or surprising that you find in the passage? Do you find anything especially challenging?

→ Are you being called to respond or take action in any way?

PRAY

Holy God, in our lament and despair, we decry the evil of empire that perpetuates such violence, injustice, and suffering. Oh Lord, we cry to you; do not let our eyes stray from the unimaginable pain and loss but help us see your presence incarnated in places of suffering, particularly Gaza. Emmanuel, born among the rubble, you stand with the oppressed and brokenhearted. We ask for your divine justice to prevail and for your light to touch the people of Gaza. Renew our commitment to stand with them, to speak truth to power, and to work for the day when all people can live in peace and security.

Lord, in your mercy, hear our prayer.

EXPLORE

Occupied with Nonviolence: A Palestinian Woman Speaks, by Jean Zaru

THE BIBLE IS
ANTI-ZIONIST
#24
MANIFEST DESTINY

THE BIBLE IS ANTI-ZIONIST #24

WHAT SORROW AWAITS YOU WHO LIE AWAKE AT NIGHT, THINKING UP EVIL PLANS. YOU RISE AT DAWN AND HURRY TO CARRY THEM OUT, SIMPLY BECAUSE YOU HAVE THE POWER TO DO SO. WHEN YOU WANT A PIECE OF LAND, YOU FIND A WAY TO SEIZE IT. WHEN YOU WANT SOMEONE'S HOUSE, YOU TAKE IT BY FRAUD AND VIOLENCE. YOU CHEAT A MAN OF HIS PROPERTY, STEALING HIS FAMILY'S INHERITANCE.

IF YOU WOULD DO WHAT IS RIGHT, YOU WOULD FIND MY WORDS COMFORTING. YET TO THIS VERY HOUR MY PEOPLE RISE AGAINST ME LIKE AN ENEMY! YOU STEAL THE SHIRTS RIGHT OFF THE BACKS OF THOSE WHO TRUSTED YOU, MAKING THEM AS RAGGED AS MEN RETURNING FROM BATTLE. YOU HAVE EVICTED WOMEN FROM THEIR PLEASANT HOMES AND FOREVER STRIPPED THEIR CHILDREN OF ALL THAT GOD WOULD GIVE THEM. UP! BEGONE! THIS IS NO LONGER YOUR LAND AND HOME, FOR YOU HAVE FILLED IT WITH SIN AND RUINED IT COMPLETELY.

MICAH 2:1-2;7-10 (NLT)

C. "Manifest Destiny"[1] - Referencing "manifest destiny," evangelical activist Jim Wallis once wrote that "the United States of America was established as a white society, founded upon the near genocide of another race and then the enslavement of yet another."

Of this, Historian John Fea explains, "Manifest Destiny was deeply informed by the long-standing evangelical idea that white Protestant 'civilization' must advance Westward. God gave the continent to Christians and it was their 'destiny' to conquer and tame it. This entire project was drenched in the unholy mix of evangelical Protestantism and white supremacy."

Beyond North America, similar theologies held sway in ***settler-colonial*** societies from Australia to Argentina. Likewise, the Afrikaner Calvinists of South Africa understood their settler-colonial project as a direct calling from God. As Mitri Raheb explains, "The permanent settlement of colonists in an occupied land is the main feature that distinguishes settler colonialism from classical or neocolonialism. The settler colonialists establish and enforce state sovereignty and juridical control over the indigenous land, ultimately aiming to eliminate the native people."

"To defend the settled property from the 'savage,'" Raheb continues, "a police state is created and is granted extraordinary power over the native people."[2]

In its most basic form, manifest destiny seeks—in the name of God and progress—to conquer, cleanse, and colonize. In the Arab context, French colonization of Algeria was immensely destructive to the native Algerians, subjecting them to a level of colonial violence that would permanently alter the region's social fabric.

Zionism, a settler-colonial theology *par excellence*, has been absolutely catastrophic to the lives, property, and psyche of the native Palestinians. Christian Zionism—from the Balfour Declaration of 1917 to the Biden Presidency and beyond—has provided theological justification, financial capital, and political cover for decades of land confiscation, ethnic cleansing, settlement activity, apartheid and, as I write, genocide.

"Our very understanding of God, our witness to the gospel, and the credibility of the Christian church," asserts Colin Chapman, "are at stake when it comes to our theology of Palestine."[3] Speaking as a western Christian, there is far too much blood on our hands, because bad theology kills.

REFLECT

→ Prayerfully read through the verses one more time. Is there a particular word, phrase, or idea that captures your attention?

→ Is there anything new or surprising that you find in the passage? Do you find anything especially challenging?

→ Are you being called to respond or take action in any way?

PRAY

God of the Oppressed, we cry out against the theologies of empire and Christian Zionism that twist your word to justify oppression. Tear down the walls of all ideologies that seek to replace your kingdom of justice and peace with systems of radicalization and domination. We pray for repentance and guidance of those in power who weaponize your name to displace the vulnerable and harm the innocent. Awaken all hearts to your boundless love and to the truth that your promises are for all people.

Lord, in your mercy, hear our prayer.

EXPLORE

Justice on the Cross: Palestinian Liberation Theology, the Struggle against Israeli Oppression, and the Church, by Kathleen Christison

THE BIBLE IS ANTI-ZIONIST

#25 THE GOD WHO SEES

NOW SARAI, ABRAM'S WIFE, HAD BORNE HIM NO CHILDREN. AND SHE HAD AN EGYPTIAN MAIDSERVANT WHOSE NAME WAS HAGAR. SO SARAI SAID TO ABRAM, "SEE NOW, THE LORD HAS RESTRAINED ME FROM BEARING CHILDREN. PLEASE, GO IN TO MY MAID; PERHAPS I SHALL OBTAIN CHILDREN BY HER" . . . WHEN HAGAR SAW THAT SHE HAD CONCEIVED, HER MISTRESS BECAME DESPISED IN HER EYES.

THEN SARAI SAID TO ABRAM, "THE WRONG DONE TO ME BE UPON YOU! I GAVE MY MAID INTO YOUR EMBRACE; AND WHEN SHE SAW THAT SHE HAD CONCEIVED, I BECAME DESPISED IN HER EYES. THE LORD JUDGE BETWEEN YOU AND ME."

SO ABRAM SAID TO SARAI, "INDEED YOUR MAID IS IN YOUR HAND; DO TO HER AS YOU PLEASE." AND WHEN SARAI DEALT HARSHLY WITH HER, SHE FLED FROM HER PRESENCE.

NOW THE ANGEL OF THE LORD FOUND HER BY A SPRING OF WATER IN THE WILDERNESS, BY THE SPRING ON THE WAY TO SHUR. AND HE SAID, "HAGAR, SARAI'S MAID, WHERE HAVE YOU COME FROM, AND WHERE ARE YOU GOING?"—SHE SAID, "I AM FLEEING FROM THE PRESENCE OF MY MISTRESS SARAI."

THE BIBLE IS ANTI-ZIONIST #25

The Angel of the Lord said to her, "Return to your mistress, and submit yourself under her hand."

Then the Angel of the Lord said to her, "I will multiply your descendants exceedingly, so that they shall not be counted for multitude."
And the Angel of the Lord Said to her:

"Behold, you are with child, And you shall bear a son. You shall call his name Ishmael (God Hears), Because the Lord has heard your affliction. He shall be a wild man; His hand shall be against every man, And every man's hand against him. And he shall dwell in the presence of all his brethren."

Then she called the name of the Lord who spoke to her, You-Are-the-God-Who-Sees; for she said, "Have I also here seen Him who sees me?"

So Hagar bore Abram a son; and Abram named his son, whom Hagar bore, Ishmael.

Genesis 16:1-13 (NKJV)

Hagar, the Egyptian slave, is a clear victim of sexual assault and domestic abuse. A cursory reading might lead one to believe that God condones her exploitation, but upon inspection it becomes evident that Hagar truly puts Abraham and Sarah to shame. For Hagar is in no way just a foil, a mere plot devise "illustrating" Abraham's lack of faith. Rather, God specifically honors Hagar in profound ways:

- God pursues Hagar, calling her by name. I have personally lived in contexts where migrant domestic workers almost seem to fade into the background. Without rights or civil protections, they are often extremely vulnerable, subject to the whims of their employers, and live in profoundly dehumanizing circumstances. In pursuing and addressing Hagar by name, God rehumanizes her, honoring Hagar's intrinsic value as a beloved creation and image bearer of the Divine.

- Hagar's child is to be named Ishmael ("God hears"). When Hagar started speaking and acting "above her station," Abram and Sarai quickly silenced her, but God hears Hagar in her affliction. Rather than "giving voice to the voiceless," God is honoring the voice she already has within her.

- Hagar has the honor of being the only person in the Bible to confer a name upon God: *El Roi* ("The God Who Sees Me"). God sees Hagar, the exploited, foreign slave woman, in the midst of her vulnerability and pain. Moreover, Hagar receives the extreme honor of gazing upon the divine presence.

- God promises to multiply the descendants of Hagar, "exceedingly." Her son Ishmael would be recognized forever as the father of multitudes, an honor and blessing conferred also to Hagar. To quote Dr. Havilah Dharamraj, "Hagar moves from being a 'victimized and endangered slave woman' to becoming the 'autonomous matriarch of a nascent people.'"[1]

- Hagar begins the story as a slave. But Ishmael "shall be a wild man; His hand shall be against every man, and every man's hand against him." In context, this is a remarkable promise of freedom (although it might not be immediately clear in the English). Hagar was "under the hand" of Sarai, but Ishmael would be "under the hand" of no man. He would be free! As "a wild man," he would not be "domesticated" by slavery or exploited like a "beast of burden." Such a promise would bring great joy to Hagar.[2]

THE BIBLE IS ANTI-ZIONIST #25

In today's passage, Ishmael is described as "dwelling in the presence of his brethren." Some, however, translate the verse as "live in perpetual hostility with his brethren," resulting in an unfortunate misunderstanding. In fact, some even speak of Ishmael as being "cursed."

In popular imagination, Israelis are often equated with Isaac and Palestinians with Ishmael, with this passage being used to posit the existence of some primordial enmity between the two. "Haven't they always been fighting?" the question goes. Or, the story is used to justify Palestinian displacement.

Such associations, however, are biblically problematic: as seen, there are better ways of interpreting the passage. Moreover, they are are historically problematic: the contemporary crisis is very much a product of recent history, born of Western imperialism and Zionist settler-colonialism rather than some ancient family feud. And, they are ethnically problematic: the Indigenous Palestinian inhabitants are heirs to ALL who have come before them in the land.

Even so, there is a long biblical as well as Islamic tradition of seeing Arabs as children of Ishmael. So, it's definitely worth reflecting deeply on these foundational passages.

REFLECT

→ Prayerfully read through the verses one more time. Is there a particular word, phrase, or idea that captures your attention?

→ Is there anything new or surprising that you find in the passage? Do you find anything especially challenging?

→ Are you being called to respond or take action in any way?

PRAY

God of Justice, in witnessing such death and violence on the innocent, we cry out with the Psalmist: "O Lord, how long shall the wicked, how long shall the wicked exult? They kill the widow and the sojourner, and murder the fatherless; and they say, 'The Lord does not see; the God of Jacob does not perceive'" (Psalm 94:3, 6-7). Hear the cries of all those whose suffering is immense and whose pain goes unseen by many. Strengthen them in their despair and hold them close in their vulnerability. Let your justice shine forth so that no cry of the oppressed nor deed of the wrong doers goes unanswered.

Lord, in your mercy, hear our prayer.

EXPLORE

"Do You See What I See: The Story of Hager," by Havilah Dharamraj in *The Religious Other: A Biblical Understanding of Islam, the Qur'an and Muhammad*, edited by Martin Accad and Jonathan Andrews

See also: *Finding Hagar: God's Pursuit of a Runaway*, by Michael F. Kuhn

THE BIBLE IS
ANTI-ZIONIST
#26
RESIDENT ALIENS

THE BIBLE IS ANTI-ZIONIST #26

SARAH TURNED TO ABRAHAM AND DEMANDED, "GET RID OF THAT SLAVE WOMAN AND HER SON. HE IS NOT GOING TO SHARE THE INHERITANCE WITH MY SON, ISAAC. I WON'T HAVE IT!"

THIS UPSET ABRAHAM VERY MUCH BECAUSE ISHMAEL WAS HIS SON. BUT GOD TOLD ABRAHAM, "DO NOT BE UPSET OVER THE BOY AND YOUR SERVANT. DO WHATEVER SARAH TELLS YOU, FOR ISAAC IS THE SON THROUGH WHOM YOUR DESCENDANTS WILL BE COUNTED. BUT I WILL ALSO MAKE A NATION OF THE DESCENDANTS OF HAGAR'S SON BECAUSE HE IS YOUR SON, TOO."

SO ABRAHAM GOT UP EARLY THE NEXT MORNING, PREPARED FOOD AND A CONTAINER OF WATER, AND STRAPPED THEM ON HAGAR'S SHOULDERS. THEN HE SENT HER AWAY WITH THEIR SON, AND SHE WANDERED AIMLESSLY IN THE WILDERNESS OF BEERSHEBA.

WHEN THE WATER WAS GONE, SHE PUT THE BOY IN THE SHADE OF A BUSH. THEN SHE WENT AND SAT DOWN BY HERSELF ABOUT A HUNDRED YARDS AWAY. "I DON'T WANT TO WATCH THE BOY DIE," SHE SAID, AS SHE BURST INTO TEARS.

BUT GOD HEARD THE BOY CRYING, AND THE ANGEL OF GOD CALLED TO HAGAR FROM HEAVEN, "HAGAR, WHAT'S WRONG? DO NOT BE AFRAID!

THE BIBLE IS ANTI-ZIONIST #26

"GOD HAS HEARD THE BOY CRYING AS HE LIES THERE. GO TO HIM AND COMFORT HIM, FOR I WILL MAKE A GREAT NATION FROM HIS DESCENDANTS."

THEN GOD OPENED HAGAR'S EYES, AND SHE SAW A WELL FULL OF WATER. SHE QUICKLY FILLED HER WATER CONTAINER AND GAVE THE BOY A DRINK. AND GOD WAS WITH THE BOY AS HE GREW UP IN THE WILDERNESS. HE BECAME A SKILLFUL ARCHER, AND HE SETTLED IN THE WILDERNESS OF PARAN. HIS MOTHER ARRANGED FOR HIM TO MARRY A WOMAN FROM THE LAND OF EGYPT.

ABOUT THIS TIME, ABIMELECH CAME WITH PHICOL, HIS ARMY COMMANDER, TO VISIT ABRAHAM. "GOD IS OBVIOUSLY WITH YOU, HELPING YOU IN EVERYTHING YOU DO," ABIMELECH SAID. "SWEAR TO ME IN GOD'S NAME THAT YOU WILL NEVER DECEIVE ME, MY CHILDREN, OR ANY OF MY DESCENDANTS. I HAVE BEEN LOYAL TO YOU, SO NOW SWEAR THAT YOU WILL BE LOYAL TO ME AND TO THIS COUNTRY WHERE YOU ARE LIVING AS A FOREIGNER."

ABRAHAM REPLIED, "YES, I SWEAR TO IT!" . . . AND ABRAHAM LIVED AS A FOREIGNER IN PHILISTINE COUNTRY FOR A LONG TIME.

GENESIS 21:10-24,34 (NLT)

It is impossible to fully understand the story of Abraham and his youngest son, Isaac, apart from the story of Hagar and Ishmael, Abraham's eldest.

In fact, Hagar's exile (in Ch. 21) is followed immediately (in Ch. 22) by God's command that Abraham kill Isaac as a sacrifice. (The child would be rescued at the last minute and replaced with a sacrificial ram.) In fact, the two stories are inseparably linked in Jewish tradition, within the annual *Rosh Hashanah* (Jewish New Year) liturgy.

Presented as parallel narratives, these are twin passages that cannot be read in isolation: As Abraham casts Ishmael away to die in the wilderness, God commands the sacrifice of Isaac. Yet, as God intervenes to save one, so too does God save the other. Just as a divine promise is made to one, so too is a divine promise made to the other.

Moreover, the Bible tells us that "God was with the boy in the wilderness," the first person about whom this is said.[1] In the story of Isaac, we are seeing a precursor to what would become the system of temple sacrifices. With Ishmael, God directly chooses to dwell ("tabernacle") together with him, the exiled and disinherited son, in the desert. In this, we find the heart of God.

This story should lead us to challenge those popular misconceptions that pit Isaac and Ishmael—or their descendants— against each other, as well as those who would use it to predict or justify present-day conflicts. To those who say Ishmael is "cursed," the passage informs us that he was anything but.

Furthermore, there is an important irony in the narrative. Abraham, we read, was entirely dependent on the hospitality of Abimelech, the Philistine, and referred to himself in Hebrew as *haggār*. According to Dr. Havilah Dharamraj, the word *haggār* (of the root *gēr*) refers to the "resident alien, the 'class of people who occupy the intermediate position between the native and the complete foreigner.' The Egyptian slave and the Mesopotamian chieftain are 'resident aliens' in Canaan, aurally linked: one's name is 'Hagar'; the other describes himself as *haggār*."[2] One is treated as an honored guest; the other is used, abused, and cast aside.

As Genesis concludes, the family of Abraham migrates to Egypt to escape famine. Generations later, Exodus begins with the story of their enslavement. Recalling Hagar's abuse, this is an intentional juxtaposition and power inversion that's difficult to ignore. The slave is set free, the master enslaved.

The story of Abraham and Hagar is a reminder that power and privilege are fickle things. Therefore, "in everything, do unto others as you would have others do unto you!" For, as Jesus tells us, "this ***IS*** the law and prophets" (Matthew 7:12).

Ultimately, Dharamraj is led to conclude that the text, as arranged, offers "a sustained and serious biblical reflection on 'the other.' What does it [take] for different peoples to live alongside one another, either sharing borders or even tents?' It takes a discerning eye.

"If only Abraham had been able to see himself in Abimelech—a man receptive of and responsive to God's instructions. If only Sarah had been able to see in Hagar a fellow foreigner."[3]

Zionists will look to the stories of Abraham to justify their conquest of the the land and the removal of its indigenous people. However, the twin stories of Abraham and Hagar, together with Isaac and Ishmael, demand serious introspection and truly lead to the exact opposite conclusion!

REFLECT

→ Prayerfully read through the verses one more time. Is there a particular word, phrase, or idea that captures your attention?

→ Is there anything new or surprising that you find in the passage? Do you find anything especially challenging?

→ Are you being called to respond or take action in any way?

PRAY

Lord, you offer freedom to all people. We seek comfort in you as we pray for those kidnapped, detained, and abused. Holy Spirit, console the thousands of current detainees and console them and their families. Holy God, we ask you to break the bonds of violence and occupation and to let your love be known even in the depths of suffering.

Lord, in your mercy, hear our prayer.

EXPLORE

Arabs in the Shadow of Israel: The Unfolding of God's Prophetic Plan for Ishmael's Line, by Tony Maalouf

THE BIBLE IS ANTI-ZIONIST

#27

REFUSING SILENCE

THE BIBLE IS ANTI-ZIONIST #27

GABRIEL APPEARED TO MARY AND SAID, "GREETINGS, FAVORED WOMAN! THE LORD IS WITH YOU!"

CONFUSED AND DISTURBED, MARY TRIED TO THINK WHAT THE ANGEL COULD MEAN. "DON'T BE AFRAID, MARY," THE ANGEL TOLD HER, "FOR YOU HAVE FOUND FAVOR WITH GOD! YOU WILL CONCEIVE AND GIVE BIRTH TO A SON, AND YOU WILL NAME HIM JESUS. HE WILL BE VERY GREAT AND WILL BE CALLED THE SON OF THE MOST HIGH. THE LORD GOD WILL GIVE HIM THE THRONE OF HIS ANCESTOR DAVID. AND HE WILL REIGN OVER JACOB FOREVER; HIS KINGDOM WILL NEVER END!"

MARY ASKED THE ANGEL, "BUT HOW CAN THIS HAPPEN? I AM A VIRGIN."—THE ANGEL REPLIED, "THE HOLY SPIRIT WILL COME UPON YOU, AND THE POWER OF THE MOST HIGH WILL OVERSHADOW YOU. SO THE BABY TO BE BORN WILL BE HOLY, AND HE WILL BE CALLED THE SON OF GOD.

MARY RESPONDED, "I AM THE LORD'S SERVANT. MAY EVERYTHING YOU HAVE SAID ABOUT ME COME TRUE."

LUKE 1:28-35,38 (NLT)

In art and literature, Mary is too often depicted as a meek and ultimately passive participant in the divine plan. "Virgin Mary, meek and mild," the song tells us. Nothing, however, is further from the truth.

Rather, hers is the story of an intrepid young woman, who, upon being presented with an otherwise impossible situation as an unmarried woman in first-century Palestine, chose to risk everything—even her very life—for the sake of God's reign and the world's liberation.

Taking upon herself and embracing the inevitable shame that could have so easily extinguished the light she carried within her, Mary would eventually become the most honored woman in history. She is a proactive, selfless actor in the Christmas story with full agency.[1]

As I consider Mary's story in light of present-day realities in the Holy Land, as we grieve with all our souls this modern-day massacre of the holy innocents in Gaza and the wider region, I cannot help but remember that Palestinians, like Mary, have far too often been silenced, written out of their own story.

THE BIBLE IS ANTI-ZIONIST #27

We are inundated with nonsensical phrases like:

"A land without a people, for a people without a land" - "There is no such thing as a Palestinian." - "Israeli-Arab" - "Israel made the desert bloom." - "There never was a Palestinian state" - "Judea and Samaria" - "Terrorist" - "Self-Defense" - "Ceasefire."

In what amounts to "epistemological genocide," such statements represent an attempt to cleanse our contemporary language and historical narratives of any reference to the Indigenous Palestinians, the living stones of the Holy Land and literal descendants of the very first followers of Jesus.

It's an attempt to extricate Palestinians not just from their own land, but from their own stories, to silence their voices, as Mary has so often been silenced.

We have been witnessing the fruit of this erasure now in Gaza. Likewise, we find partition plans and "peace accords" being concocted and proclaimed in foreign capitals and far away newsrooms, without input from the people on the ground most impacted.

THE BIBLE IS ANTI-ZIONIST #27

And yet, the Palestinians never seem to "get the message." They refuse to disappear or go away, reasserting themselves back into their narratives and global discourses, standing firm upon the justice of their cause.

Against all odds, the stories, images, and videos from Gaza have kept coming. In the diaspora, too, city after city, we find intrepid young activists leading demonstrations and engaging in nonviolent direct action, popular education, and political advocacy—often at great personal risk—secure in the justice of their cause.

Like Mary, these are women and men of agency, in whose liberation is bound our very own. It is for this reason that non-Palestinians like me, in our advocacy efforts, must stand alongside our Palestinian siblings, hearing and amplifying their stories, centering and elevating their voices, and ultimately taking from them our cues—leveraging what privilege we might have to run interference, educate our communities, and engage in the advocacy requested of us.

REFLECT

→ Prayerfully read through the verses one more time. Is there a particular word, phrase, or idea that captures your attention?

→ Is there anything new or surprising that you find in the passage? Do you find anything especially challenging?

→ Are you being called to respond or take action in any way?

PRAY

Holy God, we understand the cries of Mary through the cries of Palestinian mothers throughout the Holy Land. Help us to live out the words she proclaimed in the Magnificat: "My soul proclaims the greatness of the Lord, my spirit rejoices in God my Savior . . . He has cast down the mighty from their thrones, and has lifted up the lowly. He has filled the hungry with good things, and the rich he has sent away empty."

Lord, in your mercy, hear our prayer.

EXPLORE

Spring of Living Waters: A Theological Ethnography of Palestinian Liberation Theology: The Liberative Faith Practices of Women and Laypeople at Sabeel, by Marie-Claire Klassen

Calligraphy by Dr. Wageeh Mikhail[2]

Luke 1:33: "And he will reign over Jacob's descendants forever; his kingdom will never end."

FREE PALESTINE
THE BIBLE IS
ANTI-ZIONIST
#28
REFUSING FALSE COMFORT
peacemakers,
will be called children
of God Matthew 5:9

THE BIBLE IS ANTI-ZIONIST #28

WHEN THEY HAD GONE, AN ANGEL OF THE LORD APPEARED TO JOSEPH IN A DREAM. "GET UP," HE SAID, "TAKE THE CHILD AND HIS MOTHER AND ESCAPE TO EGYPT. STAY THERE UNTIL I TELL YOU, FOR HEROD IS GOING TO SEARCH FOR THE CHILD TO KILL HIM."

WHEN HEROD REALIZED THAT HE HAD BEEN OUTWITTED BY THE MAGI, HE WAS FURIOUS, AND HE GAVE ORDERS TO KILL ALL THE BOYS IN BETHLEHEM AND ITS VICINITY WHO WERE TWO YEARS OLD AND UNDER, IN ACCORDANCE WITH THE TIME HE HAD LEARNED FROM THE MAGI.

THEN WHAT WAS SAID THROUGH THE PROPHET JEREMIAH WAS FULFILLED: "A VOICE IS HEARD IN AL RAM, WEEPING AND GREAT MOURNING, RAHIL WEEPING FOR HER CHILDREN AND REFUSING TO BE COMFORTED, BECAUSE THEY ARE NO MORE."

MATTHEW 2:13,16-18 (NIV)

THE BIBLE IS ANTI-ZIONIST #28

Perhaps I'm being unfair, even a bit of a Scrooge, but as I reflect on the annual holiday season, it is a time when I find myself inundated with manufactured emotion, saccharine sentimentality, and consumerist excess. Even so, we must not be lulled into forgetting that the true story of Christmas is a story steeped in unspeakable violence.

With the visit of the Magi (Zoroastrian priests), King Herod is confronted with the illegitimacy of his position as Rome's imperial puppet in Jerusalem, and he lashes out in a genocidal rage worthy of Pharoah himself. In this act, he becomes the Biblical embodiment of evil and imperial violence.[1] The contemporary parallels would be uncanny, if they weren't so horrifying.

The Herods of our time and their imperial patrons must never be allowed to silence the cries of the innocent. We must continue to hear their cry, refusing to be comforted by the lies and enticements of privilege; we must amplify their plea, ensuring that the powerful be forever haunted by the cries of their victims.

When the Magi read the words of the prophets, they found hope, seeing in them the promise of new life, of deliverance and liberation.

Herod, meanwhile, instrumentalizes the very same prophecies to enact unimaginable terror in an attempt to prolong his idolatrous reign. Again, I can't help but notice the contemporary parallels.

The court prophets of Christian Zionism continue to subvert the promises of Christ's reign, as they provide ideological cover for imperial violence and settler-colonial conquest.

We must hear the cry of the holy innocents and cut through the noise of the imperial propagandists and genocide apologists who work hard to silence (even justify!) the screams of the children.

Like the mothers of Bethlehem, we must refuse to "be comforted" in the face of genocidal evil.

peacemakers, for they will be called children of God Matthew 5

REFLECT

→ Prayerfully read through the verses one more time. Is there a particular word, phrase, or idea that captures your attention?

→ Is there anything new or surprising that you find in the passage? Do you find anything especially challenging?

→ Are you being called to respond or take action in any way?

PRAY

God of Refuge, we know you are present with the displaced and see the suffering of all. We thus come before you in sorrow as we witness mounting hardships facing those who have lost both home and homeland. Hear the voices of the Palestinian refugees who yearn for stability, who desire safety, who long for a future free from fear. We ask you to intervene for the protection of all UNRWA and other aid workers and the people they serve. We pray for a softening of hearts among those in power who make decisions affecting countless lives, the end to occupation, and the respect of international law. Lord, transform structures of oppression, and dismantle barriers to justice.

Lord, in your mercy, hear our prayer.

EXPLORE

Christ in the Rubble: Faith, the Bible, and the Genocide in Gaza, by Munther Isaac

Artist: Eva Carballeira R (@evesketches)

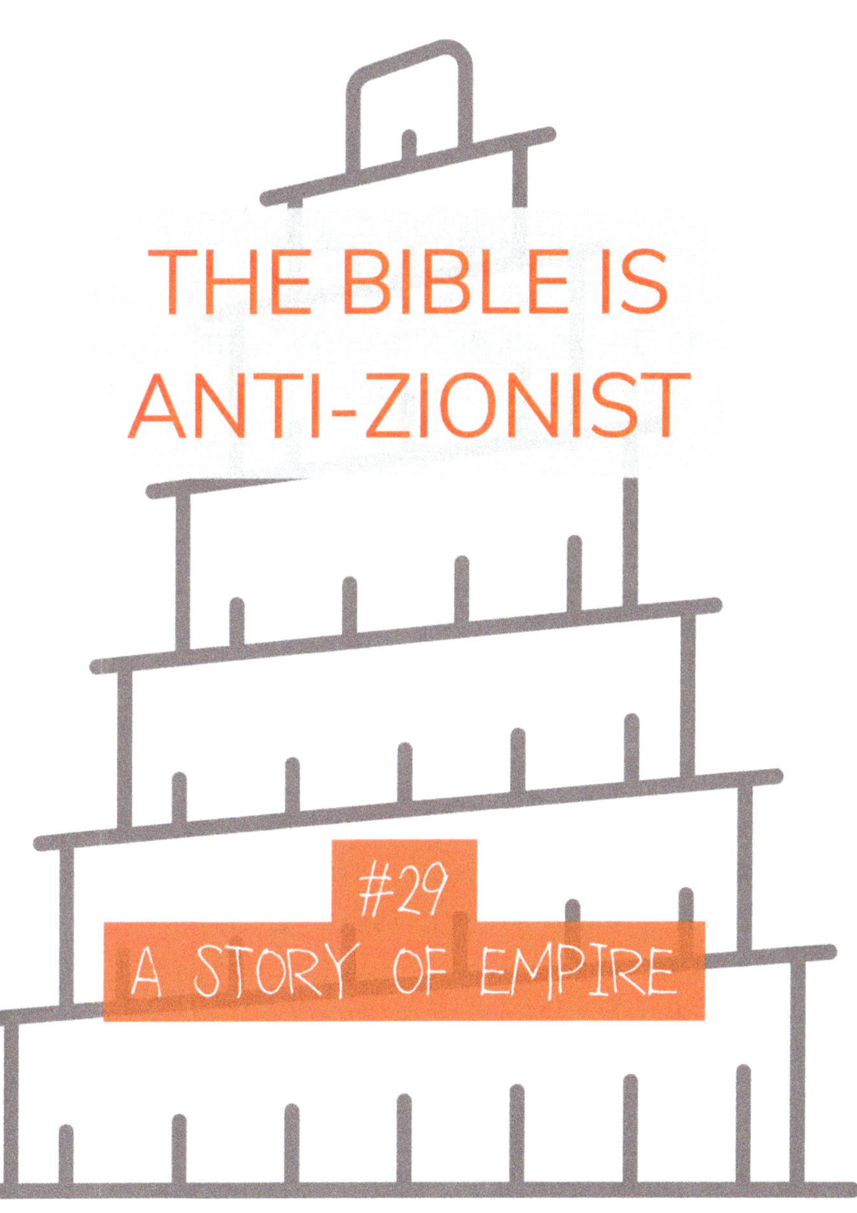

THE BIBLE IS ANTI-ZIONIST

#29 A STORY OF EMPIRE

THE BIBLE IS ANTI-ZIONIST #29

At one time all the people of the world spoke the same language and used the same words. As the people migrated to the east, they found a plain in the land of Babylonia and settled there. They began saying to each other, "Let's make bricks and harden them with fire" . . . Then they said, "Come, let's build a great city for ourselves with a tower that reaches into the sky. This will make us famous and keep us from being scattered all over the world."

But the Lord came down to look at the city and the tower the people were building. "Look!" he said. "The people are united, and they all speak the same language. After this, nothing they set out to do will be impossible for them! Come, let's go down and confuse the people with different languages. Then they won't be able to understand each other." In that way, the Lord scattered them all over the world, and they stopped building the city.

Genesis 11:1-9 (NLT)

The Tower of Babel is, at its core, a story of empire. As a clear reference to the Temple of Marduk in the heart of Babylon, it is specifically a story about the evils of imperial religion. Comparative theologian Ida Glaser speaks of "the dangerous triangle" that constitutes imperial religion, namely: people, power, and land—a volatile combination engendering immense historical conflict and human suffering.[1]

These three elements aren't inherently dangerous. In the garden, God places humanity within a specific land and grants them responsibility for its care. Glaser explains, "At the center of this triangle is God who made the people and the land, and who is the source of all power."[2] The land belonged to God, and all power was to be exercised under God's authority for the flourishing of creation.

Soon, humanity attempts to usurp God, using "the fruit of the land to gain power" and "define good and evil for themselves." This is what we see in Babel, as "the people sought to make a name for themselves." According to Glaser, "The center and the symbol of their enterprise was the tower they tried to build up to heaven. It was a religious enterprise, using religion to develop the power to keep the people in the land."[3]

Thus, imperial religion is born, the heart of which is self-idolatry and the abuse of power. "Putting religion at the center of the triangle," writes Glaser, "makes it so dangerous that God has to act in judgement."[4]

Recalling Babylon, we see the ancient kings utilizing religion to legitimize "the triangle of a particular people taking power over a particular land, and the god's temple [tower] was the greatest symbol of this."[5] It was a religion of conquest steeped in exploitation and violence.

In Scripture, this template echoes through the examples of Pharoah and the pre-exilic kings of Israel and Judah, who themselves came to embody the tyranny of imperial religion. Herod and Caesar embody this role in the New Testament. Personified in the character of Satan, the idolatry of imperial religion is seen most explicitly in the wilderness temptations of Jesus (Matthew 4:1-11). I would personally add Constantinian Christianity to the list, alongside far too many examples of contemporary religious nationalism across all traditions.

Ultimately, the manipulation of religious devotion to achieve and maintain power in order to claim and conquer a particular territory is in so many ways the very definition of Zionism.

REFLECT

→ Prayerfully read through the verses one more time. Is there a particular word, phrase, or idea that captures your attention?

→ Is there anything new or surprising that you find in the passage? Do you find anything especially challenging?

→ Are you being called to respond or take action in any way?

PRAY

God of Life, in a world that invests so much in violence, we look towards your example through your Son Jesus Christ, who taught us that to be faithful to you is to always honor the sanctity of life. Holy Spirit, remind us of Christ's call to be peacemakers, to turn swords into plowshares, and to choose compassion over conflict. In a time where so much is spent on destruction, we pray that the hearts of leaders may be transformed, choosing to invest in life, in peace, and in justice. May we, as your people, be instruments of your peace, standing against the systems of violence and bearing witness to the life-giving power of love.

Lord, in your mercy, hear our prayer.

EXPLORE

Genesis 1-11: Bible Commentaries from Muslim Contexts, by Ida Glaser and Anwarul Azad (series editors Ida Glaser and Martin Accad)

THE BIBLE IS ANTI-ZIONIST

#30

SHOULD YOU INHERIT THE LAND?

THE BIBLE IS ANTI-ZIONIST #30

THE LORD' S WORD CAME TO ME:

HUMAN ONE, THOSE WHO LIVE AMONG THOSE RUINS IN ISRAEL' S FERTILE LAND ARE SAYING, " ABRAHAM WAS JUST ONE MAN, AND HE INHERITED THE LAND. WE ARE MANY, SO CERTAINLY THE LAND HAS BEEN GIVEN TO US AS AN INHERITANCE."

SO SAY TO THEM, THE LORD GOD PROCLAIMS: YOU EAT WITH THE BLOOD, YOU LIFT YOUR EYES TO THE IDOLS, AND YOU SHED BLOOD. SHOULD YOU INHERIT THE LAND? YOU LIVE BY THE SWORD, YOU OBSERVE DETESTABLE PRACTICES, AND EVERY ONE OF YOU DEFILES HIS NEIGHBOR' S WIFE.

SHOULD YOU INHERIT THE LAND?

EZEKIEL 33:23-26 (CEB)

The Israeli government made the following argument as part of a 2018 case before the Israeli Supreme Court, illustrating its position on the topic of international law: "It is within the authority of the Government of Israel to annex any territory. [The Israeli Parliament] may ignore directives of international law in any area it pleases."[1]

Not only does this illustrate the violence and Israeli exceptionalism inherent to Zionism, but it is legally incorrect and theologically problematic. If anything, those who would lay claim to the benefits of the land covenant are subject to greater moral and ethical demands than even those required by international law.

"Contrary to popular assumption," Dr. Stephen Sizer tells us, "the Scriptures repeatedly insist that the land belongs to God and that residence was always conditional."[2]

We saw this previously when reflecting upon Leviticus 25:23. "The land must not be sold permanently, because the land is mine and you reside in my land as foreigners and strangers," nullifying Zionist claims to perpetual ownership.

Referencing Ezekiel 33, Sizer writes, "It seems the Lord anticipated the reasoning of those who arrogantly claimed unconditional right to the land because of the covenant originally made with Abraham."[3]

In recent history, the Geneva Conventions were ratified in direct response to the horrors of the Second World War, to ensure such evils never again happen. But, for international humanitarian law to make sense, basic rights must be universal in scope and application. For this reason, Zionist disdain for international law is heartbreaking. Likewise, Christian Zionist disdain for international law, the historic roots of which are deeply theological, is a tragic irony of recent history.

From its inception, Israel has been the Achilles heel of the international system, but we are now witnessing, in real time, the collapse of the post-war dream. "Rather than abide by these rules," as stated in a recent report from the United Nations OHCHR, "Israel has openly defied international law time and again, inflicting maximum suffering on civilians in the occupied Palestinian territory and beyond."[4] In Gaza, we are witnessing a live-streamed genocide, eroding the foundations of humanitarian law like nothing before. And now, the people of Lebanon, Iran, and beyond are suffering the consequences of this catastrophic collapse. How soon until it reaches us all?

REFLECT

→ Prayerfully read through the verses one more time. Is there a particular word, phrase, or idea that captures your attention?

→ Is there anything new or surprising that you find in the passage? Do you find anything especially challenging?

→ Are you being called to respond or take action in any way?

PRAY

God of Peace, we live in fear of ongoing instability and the spreading of violence across the region. In a world where belief in international law and human rights has been shattered, we ask you to bring light and healing to us. Lord, bring willingness and urgency to those in power to end the suffering of civilians and pursue a vision of human rights. Renew the spirit of all who seek accountability, and soften all hearts that peace may prevail and suffering may end.

Lord, in your mercy, hear our prayer.

EXPLORE

The Truth Shall Set You Free: The Story of a Palestinian Human Rights Lawyer Working for Peace and Justice in Palestine/Israel, by Jonathan Kuttab

THE BIBLE IS ANTI-ZIONIST

#31

THE RAPTURE DOES NOT EXIST

THE BIBLE IS ANTI-ZIONIST #31

SIBLINGS, WE WANT YOU TO KNOW ABOUT PEOPLE WHO HAVE FALLEN ASLEEP SO THAT YOU WON'T MOURN LIKE OTHERS WHO DON'T HAVE ANY HOPE. SINCE WE BELIEVE THAT JESUS DIED AND ROSE, SO WE ALSO BELIEVE THAT GOD WILL BRING WITH HIM THOSE WHO HAVE DIED IN JESUS.

WHAT WE ARE SAYING IS A MESSAGE FROM THE LORD: WE WHO ARE ALIVE AND STILL AROUND AT THE LORD'S COMING DEFINITELY WON'T GO AHEAD OF THOSE WHO HAVE DIED. THIS IS BECAUSE THE LORD HIMSELF WILL COME DOWN FROM HEAVEN WITH THE SIGNAL OF A SHOUT BY THE HEAD ANGEL AND A BLAST ON GOD'S TRUMPET.

FIRST, THOSE WHO ARE DEAD IN CHRIST WILL RISE. THEN, WE WHO ARE LIVING AND STILL AROUND WILL BE TAKEN UP TOGETHER WITH THEM IN THE CLOUDS TO MEET WITH THE LORD IN THE AIR. THAT WAY WE WILL ALWAYS BE WITH THE LORD. SO ENCOURAGE EACH OTHER WITH THESE WORDS.

1 THESSALONIANS 4:13-18 (CEB)

Few modern-day doctrines have been as destructive as "the rapture," the popular notion that the faithful will be snatched away to heaven in the blink of an eye as the sinners who remain below rightly succumb to their apocalyptic fate.

Mercifully, the rapture is not real.[1]

Simply typing out those words is remarkably therapeutic; speaking honestly, the trauma of living in continual fear of being "left behind" and left alone leaves emotional scars from which one does not quickly recover.

Moreover, such "vacuum-cleaner theologies," in general, have resulted in a specific type of apocalyptic nihilism with devastating consequences:

1. Environmental stewardship, our first ever command in the Garden, becomes instead "a rejection of God's plan." As the logic goes: "What's the point of caring for a doomed planet?"

2. Kingdom imperatives like the pursuit of justice and peace are seen as pointless in a "doomed" world, a distraction from our "true calling to save as many souls for the rapture as possible!" As a result, Christian witness can become little more than a marketing scheme.

3. Too often our human siblings, whom we are commanded to love, become expendable pawns, at best, or demonized as minions of evil, at worst. (Israelis and Palestinians, respectively.)

4. Instability and war are practically welcomed, a mere sign of the times. In fact, a US military commander recently proclaimed that President Trump was "anointed by Jesus to light the signal fire in Iran to cause Armageddon and mark his return to Earth."[2] Conveniently, having been "raptured," Christians would have no stake in the destruction left behind.

Fortunately, 1 Thessalonians 4:13-18, the classic prooftext used in support of the rapture, is not at all about this. It was a promise of hope in the face of severe Roman persecution. In Acts 1, the angels proclaim that Jesus would one day return just as he left. In the ancient world, when the king would return from a campaign or a long journey, the people went out to greet him on the road, celebrating the king's return before accompanying him back into the city.[3] As it happens, this is the very same process described in the Gospels as Palm Sunday.

Again, the rapture is not real, for the Earth—renewed, reconciled, and restored (not destroyed!)—becomes the very temple of God and the locus of God's reign (Revelation 21).

REFLECT

→ Prayerfully read through the verses one more time. Is there a particular word, phrase, or idea that captures your attention?

→ Is there anything new or surprising that you find in the passage? Do you find anything especially challenging?

→ Are you being called to respond or take action in any way?

PRAY

God of peace, comfort all families who are mourning their loved ones. Protect their mourning from being appropriated by political agendas and assure them you see and know their pain. Lord, we plead you to stop the abusive power games by empires who cause so many lives to be lost.

Lord, in your mercy, hear our prayer.

EXPLORE

The Rise and Fall of Dispensationalism: How the Evangelical Battle over the End Times Shaped a Nation, by Daniel Hummel

THE BIBLE IS ANTI-ZIONIST

#32

DISTURBING THE PEACE

THE BIBLE IS ANTI-ZIONIST #32

PAUL AND SILAS JOURNEYED THROUGH AMPHIPOLIS AND APOLLONIA, THEN CAME TO THESSALONICA . . .

BUT THE JEWISH LEADERSHIP BECAME JEALOUS AND BROUGHT ALONG SOME THUGS WHO WERE HANGING OUT IN THE MARKETPLACE. THEY FORMED A MOB AND STARTED A RIOT IN THE CITY. THEY ATTACKED JASON'S HOUSE, INTENDING TO BRING PAUL AND SILAS BEFORE THE PEOPLE. WHEN THEY DIDN'T FIND THEM, THEY DRAGGED JASON AND SOME BELIEVERS BEFORE THE CITY OFFICIALS.

THEY WERE SHOUTING, "THESE PEOPLE WHO HAVE BEEN DISTURBING THE PEACE THROUGHOUT THE EMPIRE HAVE ALSO COME HERE. WHAT IS MORE, JASON HAS WELCOMED THEM INTO HIS HOME. EVERY ONE OF THEM DOES WHAT IS CONTRARY TO CAESAR'S DECREES BY NAMING SOMEONE ELSE AS KING: JESUS." THIS PROVOKED THE CROWD AND THE CITY OFFICIALS EVEN MORE.

ACTS 17:1,5-8 (CEB)

To reiterate, the rapture does not exist. Rather, Acts 17 provides neccessary historical context for understanding Paul's letter to the Thessalonians that we examined previously.

Echoing the experience of Jesus, we see yet another instance of religious leadership allying itself with empire for the sake of maintaining power and influence. In putting their faith in the false promises of Caesar they became local agents and legitimizers of imperial violence.

In 1 Thessalonians 2:14, Paul writes, "My friends, you did just like God's churches in Judea and like the other followers of Christ Jesus there. And so, you were mistreated by your own people, in the same way they were mistreated by their people" (CEV).

Acts 17 gives essential context for how and why this persecution came about and of the people's longing for the true king's return, about which Paul is writing in Thessealonians.

To proclaim the lordship of Christ is to deny, by default, the lordship of Caesar. If Christ is King, then Caesar is not!

THE BIBLE IS ANTI-ZIONIST #32

The gospel proclamation (*kerygma*) is a direct challenge to the legitimacy and lordship of Caesar "as divine representative on earth," of the total allegiance and devotion demanded from us by empire, and of the violence and exploitation inherent to the political economics of the imperial system. This likewise applies to the myriad nationalisms, totalizing ideologies, and destructive systems of modern life.

The vision and values of God's Kingdom are truly countercultural, as they run directly counter to the way of empire— naturally engendering opposition. The very existence of the early church, N.T. Wright explains, "threatened the foundational assumptions of pagan society."[1] In this lies the heart of authentic anti-Christian persecution.

Ultimately, the biblical narrative offers a sharp, liberatory critique of empire, the imperial economy, and the imperial religions animating it.

Today, Zionism and Christian Zionism, together with the growing influence of Christian Nationalism, play just such an animating role—in their complete inversion of biblical ethics and idolatrous alignment with and dependence upon the violent power of the imperial *Pax American* system.

REFLECT

→ Prayerfully read through the verses one more time. Is there a particular word, phrase, or idea that captures your attention?

→ Is there anything new or surprising that you find in the passage? Do you find anything especially challenging?

→ Are you being called to respond or take action in any way?

PRAY

God of Freedom, protect those who worship amid fear, and grant courage to those barred from sacred spaces. Soften the hearts of those in power, that they may choose mercy over oppression. Bring peace to every street and let justice flow through the land. May all worship in freedom and safety, and may peace and dignity be restored to all.

Lord, in your mercy, hear our prayer.

EXPLORE

Challenging Empire: God, Faithfulness and Resistance, edited by Naim Ateek, Cedar Duaybis, and Maurine Tobin

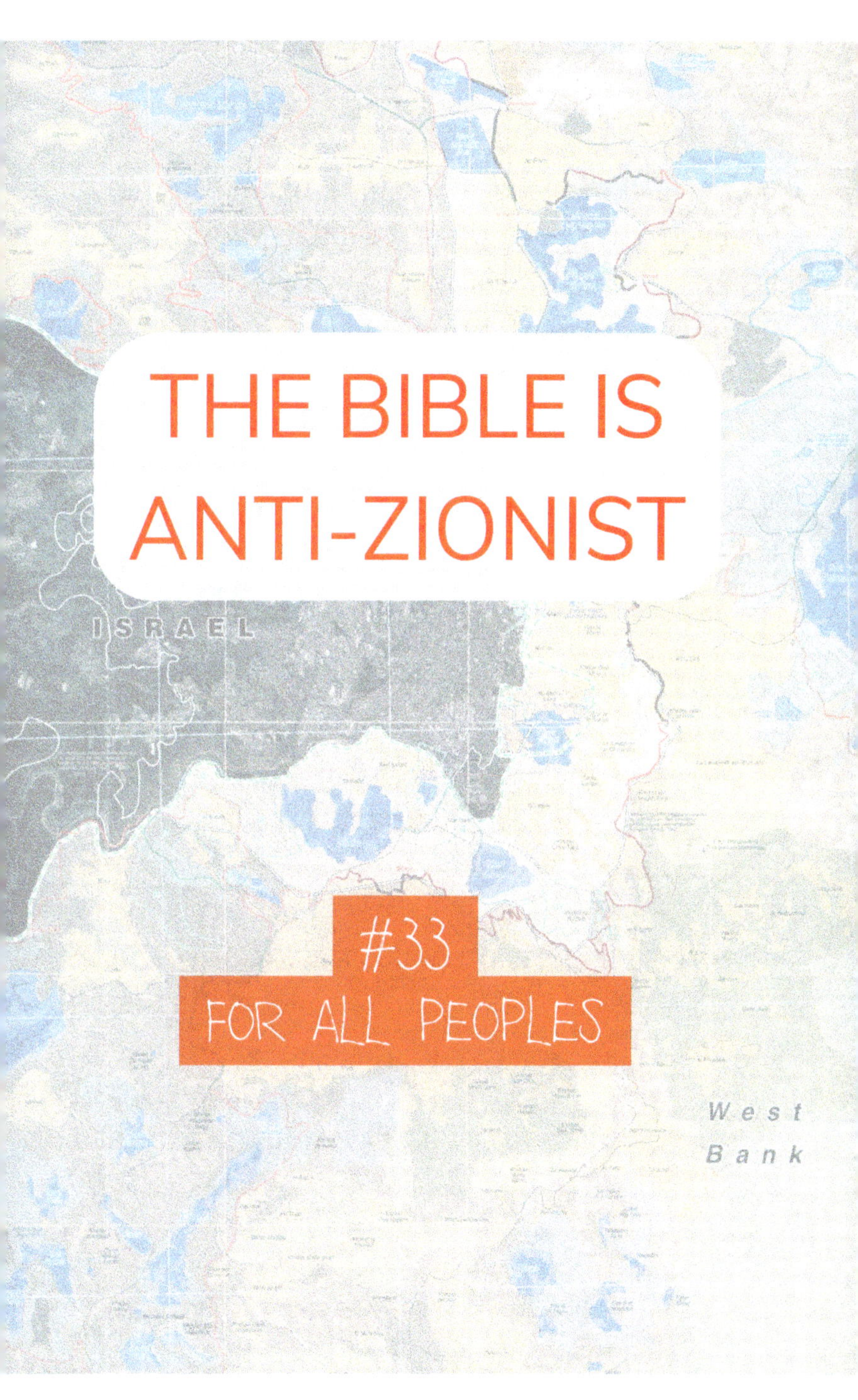
THE BIBLE IS
ANTI-ZIONIST
ISRAEL
#33
FOR ALL PEOPLES
West
Bank

DON'T LET THE STRANGER WHO HAS JOINED WITH THE LORD SAY, "THE LORD WILL EXCLUDE ME FROM THE PEOPLE." AND DON'T LET THE EUNUCH SAY, "I'M JUST A DRY TREE." THE LORD SAYS: TO THE EUNUCHS WHO KEEP MY SABBATHS, CHOOSE WHAT I DESIRE, AND REMAIN LOYAL TO MY COVENANT: IN MY TEMPLE AND COURTS, I WILL GIVE THEM A MONUMENT AND A NAME BETTER THAN SONS AND DAUGHTERS. I WILL GIVE TO THEM AN ENDURING NAME THAT WON'T BE REMOVED.

THE STRANGERS WHO HAVE JOINED ME, SERVING ME AND LOVING MY NAME, BECOMING MY SERVANTS, EVERYONE WHO KEEPS THE SABBATH WITHOUT MAKING IT IMPURE, AND THOSE WHO HOLD FAST TO MY COVENANT: I WILL BRING THEM TO MY HOLY MOUNTAIN, AND BRING THEM JOY IN MY HOUSE OF PRAYER. I WILL ACCEPT THEIR ENTIRELY BURNED OFFERINGS AND SACRIFICES ON MY ALTAR. MY HOUSE WILL BE KNOWN AS A HOUSE OF PRAYER FOR ALL PEOPLES, SAYS THE LORD GOD, WHO GATHERS ISRAEL'S OUTCASTS. I WILL GATHER STILL OTHERS TO THOSE I HAVE ALREADY GATHERED.

ISAIAH 56:3-8 (CEB)

THE BIBLE IS ANTI-ZIONIST #33

Justice for the "the stranger" is a central, frequently repeated tenet of biblical morality.

The Hebrew word for "stranger" used here by Isaiah, *nêkâr*, can very much refer to the "immigrant" or "foreigner," those having migrated from a distant land, and it is appropriately translated as such.

However, *nêkâr* need not refer to "geographical foreignness," as it can refer also to the socio-cultural "other" who nevertheless inhabits the same territorial space—in other words, the "stranger next door."[1]

In fact, English Bibles will speak of the "foreign gods of the land" when referring to what is in fact the Indigenous Canaanite religion with whom the Israelites came into contact.

Born and raised in small town California, I don't need to imagine what it's like when distinct communities live side-by-side, yet seemingly occupy entirely different socio-cultural and linguistic worlds. The situation could even be described as an "invisible apartheid" (at least from the perspective of the more privileged, fully documented, and legally protected class).

Having lived many years in Beirut, I saw too how the different religious (Christian, Sunni, Shia, Druze) and ethnic (Arab, Dom, Armenian) communities would frequently speak of and relate to each other as if they were complete foreigners. This doesn't even include multi-generation refugee communities (Palestinian, Iraqi, Syrian). Nor does it include the expansive migrant domestic worker communities.

One might also picture the way Israeli settlements encroach upon and jut up against historic Palestinian villages and neighborhoods: two vastly different worlds occupying the same geographic space, yet divided by apartheid. Moreover, I have yet to mention the frequently marginalized and excluded Bedouin communities.

"In Isaiah 56," Dr. Stephen Sizer asserts, "we see the Lord anticipate and repudiate the rise of an exclusive Israeli nationalism."[2] Truly, I am not exaggerating when I say that the Bible is anti-Zionist.

REFLECT

→ Prayerfully read through the verses one more time. Is there a particular word, phrase, or idea that captures your attention?

→ Is there anything new or surprising that you find in the passage? Do you find anything especially challenging?

→ Are you being called to respond or take action in any way?

PRAY

God of Liberation, just as your Son turned over the tables in the temple in the face of desecration, so too we ask you to stand against all acts of aggression and protect the vulnerable. Let no evil deed go unnoticed by your divine justice but rather, let your light of justice extinguish the flames and shadows of destruction. Let the cries of all the captives, detained, and displaced stir the hearts of the world, moving us to act with compassion, courage, and unwavering resolve.

Lord, in your mercy, hear our prayer.

EXPLORE

Christian Zionism: Roadmap to Armageddon? by Stephen Sizer

THE BIBLE IS ANTI-ZIONIST

#34 HOMETOWN HERO

THE BIBLE IS ANTI-ZIONIST #34

JESUS SAID "I ASSURE YOU THAT NO PROPHET IS WELCOME IN THE PROPHET'S HOMETOWN. AND I CAN ASSURE YOU THAT THERE WERE MANY WIDOWS IN ISRAEL DURING ELIJAH'S TIME, WHEN IT DIDN'T RAIN FOR THREE AND A HALF YEARS AND THERE WAS A GREAT FOOD SHORTAGE IN THE LAND. YET ELIJAH WAS SENT TO NONE OF THEM BUT ONLY TO A WIDOW IN THE CITY OF ZAREPHATH IN THE REGION OF SIDON. THERE WERE ALSO MANY PERSONS WITH SKIN DISEASES IN ISRAEL DURING THE TIME OF THE PROPHET ELISHA, BUT NONE OF THEM WERE CLEANSED. INSTEAD, NAAMAN THE SYRIAN WAS CLEANSED."

WHEN THEY HEARD THIS, EVERYONE IN THE SYNAGOGUE WAS FILLED WITH ANGER. THEY ROSE UP AND RAN HIM OUT OF TOWN. THEY LED HIM TO THE CREST OF THE HILL ON WHICH THEIR TOWN HAD BEEN BUILT SO THAT THEY COULD THROW HIM OFF THE CLIFF. BUT HE PASSED THROUGH THE CROWD AND WENT ON HIS WAY.

LUKE 4:24-30 (CEB)

More than anything else, a prophet speaks truth to power and casts an alternative vision for the way things could and should be. As such, prophets represent an inherent threat to the status quo and to those whose power and privilege depend on maintaining it. For this reason, Jesus declares, "no prophet is welcome in their hometown."

During his inaugural sermon in Luke 4, Jesus proclaims the fulfillment of Isaiah 61 as the coming of the Day of the Lord, the day of liberation. In response, the congregation is ecstatic: "Everyone was raving about Jesus, so impressed were they by the gracious words flowing from his lips. They said, 'This is Joseph's son, isn't it?'"

And yet, Jesus persisted, and within minutes his own faith community was overtaken by a murderous rage, as they attempted to throw him off the nearby cliff.

What led to such a dramatic change of heart? As we see from the text, it was the inclusion of the foreign enemy as beneficiary of divine blessing, juxtaposed with God's judgement against themselves.[1]

In doing so, Jesus, like the prophets before him, posed a challenge to their very identity as a community. Inconvenient truths can be profoundly destabilizing when they call into question the worldview and self-perception of a people group (or other marker of collective identity). "What evokes persecution," N.T. Wright tells us, "is precisely that which challenges a worldview, that which up-ends a symbolic universe."[2]

In situations of group conflict, it can get to the point where not just the words but the very existence of another is perceived as a threat to one's own identity and self-concept.

In settler-colonial societies, native voices are suppressed precisely because they challenge the foundational narratives upon which group identity is based. Exposure to such voices and narratives can be remarkably destabilizing to the psycho-emotional security of the dominant group.

Discussing the 1948 Nakba is taboo in Israeli society for this very reason, and it is why symbols of Palestinian identity are suppressed, and even why the historic existence of Palestinians is so often denied. Tragically, such acts of linguistic and intellectual erasure are far too often a prelude to the violent erasure of a people group in its entirety, to genocide.

REFLECT

→ Prayerfully read through the verses one more time. Is there a particular word, phrase, or idea that captures your attention?

→ Is there anything new or surprising that you find in the passage? Do you find anything especially challenging?

→ Are you being called to respond or take action in any way?

PRAY

Creator God, we cry out to you in anguish as voices of hatred and destruction rise once more. Lord, we name the injustice: those calling for the expulsion of Palestinians, the erasure of homes, and the pursuit of domination. Help us to embrace the truth that all your children are made in your image, worthy of life and dignity. We ask for the strength to never grow weary in the fight for justice until freedom and dignity belong to all.

Lord, in your mercy, hear our prayer.

EXPLORE

Theology of Reconciliation in the Context of Church Relations: A Palestinian Christian Perspective in Dialogue with Miroslav Volf, by Rula Khoury Mansour

THE BIBLE IS
ANTI-ZIONIST
#35
YOU HAVE HEARD IT SAID

THE BIBLE IS ANTI-ZIONIST #35

THIS IS WHAT THE LORD OF HEAVEN' S ARMIES HAS DECLARED: I HAVE DECIDED TO SETTLE ACCOUNTS WITH THE NATION OF AMALEK FOR OPPOSING ISRAEL WHEN THEY CAME FROM EGYPT. NOW GO AND COMPLETELY DESTROY THE ENTIRE AMALEKITE NATION: MEN, WOMEN, CHILDREN, BABIES, CATTLE, SHEEP, GOATS, CAMELS, AND DONKEYS."

1 SAMUEL 15:2-3 (NLT)

"YOU HAVE HEARD THE LAW THAT SAYS THE PUNISHMENT MUST MATCH THE INJURY: 'AN EYE FOR AN EYE, AND A TOOTH FOR A TOOTH.' BUT I SAY, DO NOT RESIST AN EVIL PERSON! IF SOMEONE SLAPS YOU ON THE RIGHT CHEEK, OFFER THE OTHER CHEEK ALSO. IF YOU ARE SUED IN COURT AND YOUR SHIRT IS TAKEN FROM YOU, GIVE YOUR COAT, TOO. IF A SOLDIER DEMANDS THAT YOU CARRY HIS GEAR FOR A MILE, CARRY IT TWO MILES. GIVE TO THOSE WHO ASK, AND DON'T TURN AWAY FROM THOSE WHO WANT TO BORROW.

MATTHEW 5:38-42 (NLT)

On November 4, 2023, as Israeli forces were invading Gaza, Prime Minister Benjamin Netanyahu proclaimed: "'You must remember what Amalek has done to you', says our Holy Bible. And we do remember."[1] To everyone paying attention, this reference to 1 Samuel 15 was a crystal clear declaration of genocidal intent.

As the story goes, Saul kept the Amalekite king alive, and his descendent Haman, seen in the book of Esther, would eventually seek the destruction of the Jewish people. (Tragically, when fortunes were reversed, Esther and Mordecai went on a deadly rampage of their own.[2]) As such, casting the Palestinians as "Amalek" sent an unmistakable and immediately terrifying message.

Rather than acknowledging the tragic irony inherent to such depictions of unending tit-for-tat retaliation and bloody revenge—that in attempting to destroy the other you are simply laying the groundwork for your own destruction—Israeli leaders have cherry-picked and decontextualized the most violent passages to legitimize a campaign of bloody terror throughout the Gaza Strip and beyond.

Ultimately, it's essential to recognize that the mere existence of a passage does not automatically make that passage ethically authoritative or prescriptive for us today.

It may very well be an important part of the biblical narrative, but it certainly doesn't mean we have an ethical obligation to go out and eliminate our enemies. Otherwise, anyone and anything we don't like can (and will!) become "Amalek" to us.

For the Christian, we must read and apply Scripture in light of the life and teachings of Jesus Christ.[3] And, Jesus has some pretty strong things to say about tit-for-tat retaliation and the obligation to love our enemies. So, in the words of an old bumper sticker I used to have pinned up in my office, "When Jesus said love your enemies, I think he probably meant don't kill them."

"You have heard that the law says . . ." Jesus declares, "but I say to you . . ." These divine words delivered from a Galilean hilltop, in a sermon frequently referred to as "the constitution" of the Kingdom of God, constitute our moral law as followers of Jesus Christ. We have an ethical obligation to hear these words of Jesus and put them into practice (Matthew 7:24).

REFLECT

→ Prayerfully read through the verses one more time. Is there a particular word, phrase, or idea that captures your attention?

→ Is there anything new or surprising that you find in the passage? Do you find anything especially challenging?

→ Are you being called to respond or take action in any way?

PRAY

God of Mercy, after witnessing endless massacres, the Palestinian people continue to endure unimaginable pain. We are overwhelmed by the tragic news of hundreds and hundreds of families who have been wiped from existence, while the world remains silent. Lord, we hold each and every family in our hearts, lifting them to you in prayer. May they find peace in your eternal embrace, and may their memories fuel the strength of the living to seek justice and healing.

Lord, in your mercy, hear our prayer.

EXPLORE

Justice and the Way of Jesus: Christian Ethics and the Incarnational Discipleship of Glen Stassen, edited by David P. Gushee and Reggie Williams
See also: *Gender, Genocide, Gaza and the Book of Esther: Engaging Texts of Terror(ism)*, Sarojini Nadar.

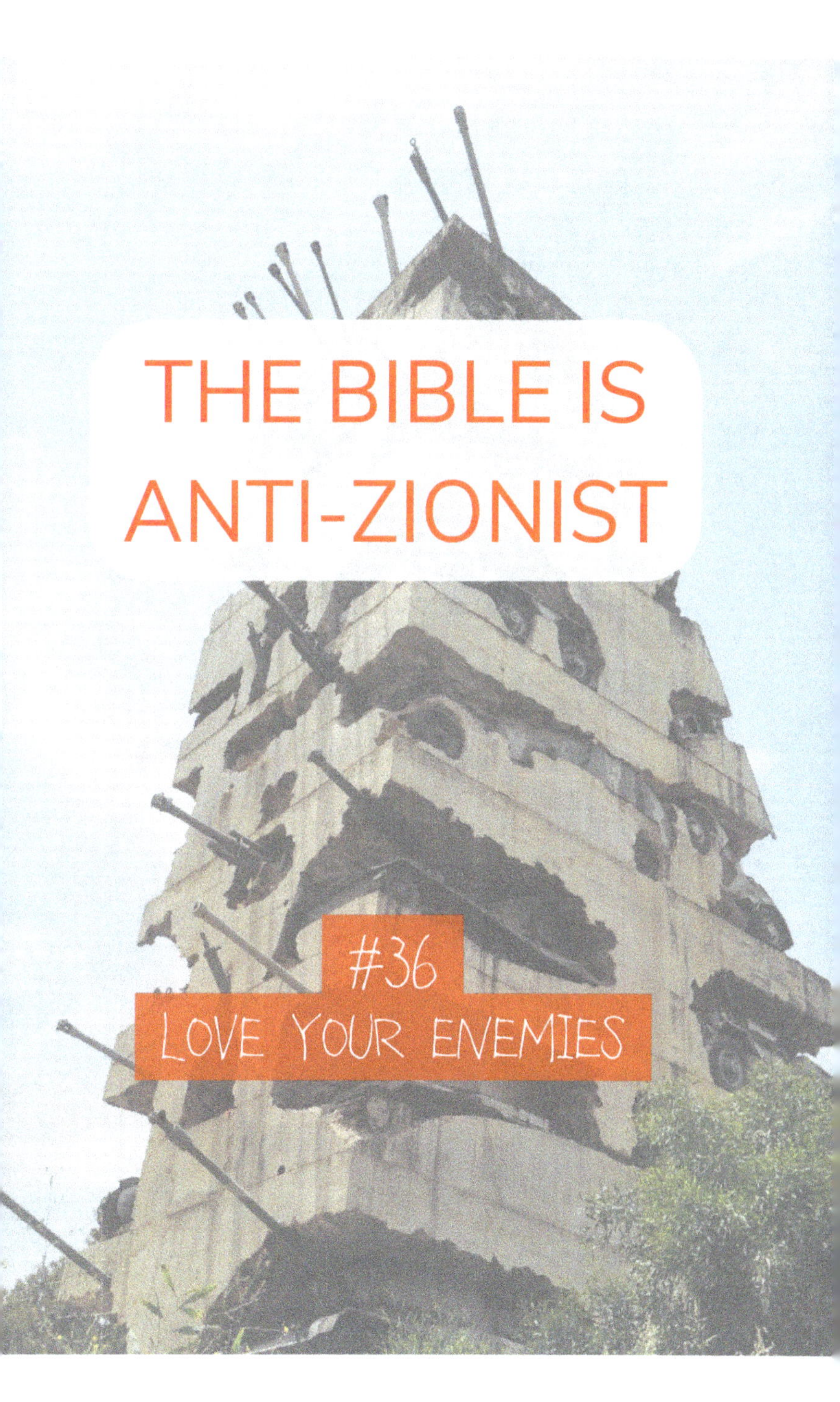
THE BIBLE IS
ANTI-ZIONIST
#36
LOVE YOUR ENEMIES

THE BIBLE IS ANTI-ZIONIST #36

PEOPLE OF ISRAEL, THE LORD YOUR GOD WILL HELP YOU TAKE THE LAND OF THE [SEVEN NATIONS] . . . WHEN YOU ATTACK THEM, THE LORD WILL FORCE THEM OUT OF THE LAND. THEN YOU MUST DESTROY THEM WITHOUT MERCY. DON'T MAKE ANY PEACE TREATIES WITH THEM, AND DON'T LET YOUR SONS AND DAUGHTERS MARRY ANY OF THEM.

DEUTERONOMY 7:1-3 (CEV)

THIS IS WHAT I SAY TO ALL WHO WILL LISTEN TO ME: **LOVE YOUR ENEMIES, AND BE GOOD TO EVERYONE WHO HATES YOU.** ASK GOD TO BLESS ANYONE WHO CURSES YOU, AND PRAY FOR EVERYONE WHO IS CRUEL TO YOU . . . IF YOU LOVE ONLY SOMEONE WHO LOVES YOU, WILL GOD PRAISE YOU FOR THAT? EVEN SINNERS LOVE PEOPLE WHO LOVE THEM. IF YOU ARE KIND ONLY TO SOMEONE WHO IS KIND TO YOU, WILL GOD BE PLEASED WITH YOU FOR THAT? . . . BUT LOVE YOUR ENEMIES AND BE GOOD TO THEM.

LUKE 6:27-28,32-33,35 (CEV)

I fully acknowledge the truth that many passages can be incredibly difficult for those of us committed to both scriptural authority and biblical justice. Moreover, it is essential to address reception history, how a text has been understood and applied over the centuries. As Dr. Mitri Raheb explains, "The Bible has been used as a tool for colonization since the sixteenth century. The land promise was used repeatedly as the pretext for land confiscation and colonization in North America, Africa, and Australia . . ."[1]

For this reason, numerous texts remain intensely distressing, terrorizing even for those victimized by their abuse. This must necessarily impact how we read and apply such passages today, and this is especially true with regard to the Palestinian experience.

Raheb continues, "Israel is no exception to this pattern and must be understood within this context of European settler colonization. When we talk about land theology, we cannot ignore the European history of colonization or shy away from the colonialist reception history of the Bible . . ."[2]

"Joshua," Raheb explains, "was the role model for Ben Gurion, Moshe Dayan, and for the many Jewish Zionist settlers who saw the book as a blueprint for their settler colonial project and the ethnic cleansing of the Palestinian people."[3]

The truth, however, is that none of these troubling texts can be read in isolation from those other passages we have already examined. Therefore, to emulate or draw inspiration from biblical depictions of violence is to make a conscious interpretive choice. It requires, by necessity, a proactive decision to reject or ignore so much else —so much beauty—contained in the pages of Scripture. As such, choosing violence reveals so much more about the contemporary reader than it does about anyone or anything else. In this way, I don't think any text can justifiably be used to support modern violence, let alone Zionism.

These are essential questions of biblical "hermeneutics," of interpretation and ethics: how are people of faith to live and act today in light of our reading and understanding of the ancient biblical texts? Different responses to this question naturally result in the diversity of traditions, schools of thought, and even distinct religions that we see today. Even so, this isn't a free for all.

There exist both responsible and deeply irresponsible ways of reading and applying Scripture. If Jesus is who we claim him to be, then I firmly believe that all scripture must be filtered through the lens of his direct teachings in the Gospels (particularly Matthew 5-7, and especially the Golden Rule). Doing so makes willfully violent applications of scripture next to impossible.

REFLECT

→ Prayerfully read through the verses one more time. Is there a particular word, phrase, or idea that captures your attention?

→ Is there anything new or surprising that you find in the passage? Do you find anything especially challenging?

→ Are you being called to respond or take action in any way?

PRAY

God of inclusivity, it is heartbreaking that your name is used to justify violence and supremacy. Illuminate how these theologies of supremacy kill, and forgive those who subscribe to Christian Zionism, unaware of its consequences: ". . . for they do not know what they are doing..." (Luke 23:34). Lord, as we call upon those who justify violence through the Christian faith to repent, help us guard ourselves against the temptation of self-righteousness.

Lord, in your mercy, hear our prayer.

EXPLORE

Theology after Gaza: A Global Anthology, edited by Mitri Raheb and Graham McGeoch

THE BIBLE IS ANTI-ZIONIST

#37

NEITHER US, NOR OUR ENEMIES

NOW WHEN JOSHUA WAS NEAR JERICHO, HE LOOKED UP AND SAW A MAN STANDING IN FRONT OF HIM WITH A DRAWN SWORD IN HIS HAND. JOSHUA WENT UP TO HIM AND ASKED, " ARE YOU FOR US OR FOR OUR ENEMIES?"

" NEITHER," HE REPLIED, " BUT AS COMMANDER OF THE ARMY OF THE LORD I HAVE NOW COME."

THEN JOSHUA FELL FACEDOWN TO THE GROUND IN REVERENCE, AND ASKED HIM, " WHAT MESSAGE DOES MY LORD HAVE FOR HIS SERVANT?"

THE COMMANDER OF THE LORD'S ARMY REPLIED, " TAKE OFF YOUR SANDALS, FOR THE PLACE WHERE YOU ARE STANDING IS HOLY." AND JOSHUA DID SO.

JOSHUA 5:13-15 (NIV)

Needless to say, the book of Joshua can be problematic. The conquest narratives can (and should!) be horrifying to contemporary ears. Joshua's reception history is steeped in Indigenous blood, frequently weaponized to justify settler-colonial violence.[1] Do I often wish it were not included in the Bible for this exact reason? Yes.

So, it is important to emphasize the fact that these conquest narratives are not ethically prescriptive—especially for Christians, who must look instead to the book of Acts as the New Testament counterpart to Joshua. Furthermore, all moral instruction must be filtered through the life, death, resurrection, and divine words of Jesus.

That being said, I want to emphasize that Joshua is impossible to properly understand, on its own terms, if not read in light of the Exile. Likely composed during the Exile, the book serves as a way for the exiles to process and come to terms with their lived trauma.

Scholars can debate questions of historical accuracy, but, in analyzing the narrative, I remain confident in my assertion that the Bible is anti-Zionist. The text itself[2] provides many clues as to why we shouldn't go out conquering in the name of God:

THE BIBLE IS ANTI-ZIONIST #37

A) The "Commander of the Lord's Armies" states explicitly that God is non-partisan. B) The people are reminded continually that the result of covenant infidelity is exile.

C) The Hebrews are merely the tools of God's judgement on the Canaanites, as the Assyrians and Babylonians would eventually be for the Israelites. D) Whenever Canaanites turn to God, they are openly welcomed, challenging any claim to ethnic privilege or exclusivity.

E) As the story progresses, we will see a stark contrast between the victory at Jericho (Ch. 6) and the defeat at Ai (Ch. 7)—highlighting the need to rely on trust and obedience, NOT military supremacy or privilege. Life and death is the province of God, not human generals.

F) In keeping with the era, the language of destruction is hyperbolic. Depictions of a group's total destruction are followed by later interactions with those very same people.

Ultimately, Joshua is limited to a distinct moment in the biblical narrative. God is enacting judgement on a specific people at a unique moment in time, but it is ALWAYS in reference to and seen through the lens of the Israelite's own destruction and exile.[3]

REFLECT

→ Prayerfully read through the verses one more time. Is there a particular word, phrase, or idea that captures your attention?

→ Is there anything new or surprising that you find in the passage? Do you find anything especially challenging?

→ Are you being called to respond or take action in any way?

PRAY

God of Justice and Compassion, we cry out for those in the Holy Land facing unjust laws and relentless oppression. We grieve for families torn from their homes and exiled. We see mothers, fathers, children stripped of their rights, their dignity trampled, and we lament for a system that punishes them for who they are. Holy Spirit, awaken the world to the suffering of those crushed beneath the weight of occupation and unjust systems. May your light shine into the darkest halls of power, and may your love bring freedom to the oppressed and courage to the persecuted.

Lord, in your mercy, hear our prayer.

EXPLORE

Theologies of Liberation in Palestine-Israel: Indigenous, Contextual, and Postcolonial Perspectives, edited by Nur Masalha and Lisa Isherwood

See also: "Refuting the Violent Image of God in the Book of Joshua 6-12," by Niveen Sarras

THE BIBLE IS ANTI-ZIONIST

#38
EMPATHY & REPENTANCE

THE BIBLE IS ANTI-ZIONIST #38

One day the Lord told Jonah, the son of Amittai, to go to the great city of Nineveh and say to the people, "The Lord has seen your terrible sins. You are doomed!" Instead, Jonah ran from the Lord. He went to the seaport of Jaffa and found a ship that was going to Spain.

Jonah 1:1-3 (CEV)

When God saw that the people had stopped doing evil things, he had pity and did not destroy them as he had planned.

Jonah was really upset and angry. So he prayed: Our Lord, I knew from the very beginning that you wouldn't destroy Nineveh. That's why I left my own country and headed for Spain. You are a kind and merciful God, and you are very patient. You always show love, and you don't like to punish anyone. Now let me die! I'd be better off dead—The Lord replied, "What right do you have to be angry?"

Jonah then left through the east gate of the city and made a shelter to protect himself from the sun. He sat under the shelter, waiting to see what would happen to Nineveh.

THE BIBLE IS ANTI-ZIONIST #38

THE LORD MADE A VINE GROW UP TO SHADE JONAH'S HEAD AND PROTECT HIM FROM THE SUN. JONAH WAS VERY HAPPY TO HAVE THE VINE, BUT EARLY THE NEXT MORNING THE LORD SENT A WORM TO CHEW ON THE VINE, AND THE VINE DRIED UP.

DURING THE DAY THE LORD SENT A SCORCHING WIND, AND THE SUN BEAT DOWN ON JONAH'S HEAD, MAKING HIM FEEL FAINT. JONAH WAS READY TO DIE, AND HE SHOUTED, "I WISH I WERE DEAD!"

BUT THE LORD ASKED, "JONAH, DO YOU HAVE THE RIGHT TO BE ANGRY ABOUT THE VINE?"—"YES, I DO," HE ANSWERED, "AND I'M ANGRY ENOUGH TO DIE."

BUT THE LORD SAID:
"YOU ARE CONCERNED ABOUT A VINE THAT YOU DID NOT PLANT OR TAKE CARE OF, A VINE THAT GREW UP IN ONE NIGHT AND DIED THE NEXT.
IN THAT CITY OF NINEVEH THERE ARE MORE THAN 120,000 PEOPLE WHO CANNOT TELL RIGHT FROM WRONG, AND MANY CATTLE ARE ALSO THERE. DON'T YOU THINK I SHOULD BE CONCERNED ABOUT THAT BIG CITY?"

JONAH 3:10-4:6-11 (CEV)

God commissions Jonah to proclaim judgement on the Assyrian city of Nineveh—capital to an empire every bit as violent and evil as Egypt or Babylon. This is the empire that would completely obliterate the Northern Kingdom of Israel in 722 BC.

But, in response to God's call, Jonah immediately flees in the opposite direction. Why?

To send a prophet with a message of judgment is actually an invitation to repent. While such messages were often aimed at the people and the leadership of Israel and Judah, the idea that God would do the same for the Assyrians was simply unacceptable to Jonah.

As Rev. Naim Ateek explains, "Jonah could not believe that God would ask him to do that. How could God even entertain the thought of sending him to preach repentance to his enemies? Why would 'his' God even care about the Assyrians, let alone seek their salvation? Should not 'his' God destroy the people of Nineveh, including its king and princes? They were his staunchest enemies and 'his' God should totally annihilate them."[1]

Even the notion that God could forgive and accept the Assyrians was just too much for Jonah to take. So, he fled. But God is not a partisan, territorial deity. Tarshish (in Spain) was not, therefore, "out of bounds." So, Jonah winds up in the belly of a great fish.

That God is a God of immeasurable grace who pursues us even in the midst of our rebellion is an important reading of the story, but stopping here leaves it incomplete.

Ultimately, the book of Jonah is an exploration of the very nature of God, the identity of God's people, the boundaries of the God's holy land, and the true scope of God's circle of care. For this reason, Rev. Ateek refers to the book of Jonah as "the theological climax" of the Hebrew Scriptures.

It is essential to note how the book of Jonah both condemns and contextualizes the prophet's hatred. One the one hand, Jonah sees the Assyrians as "human animals," dehumanized and cast out beyond the reach of his empathy. On the other hand, Jonah and his people were victims of Assyrian aggression. His kingdom was literally wiped off the face of the map.

Nevertheless, just as Assyria is being called to repent for its many crimes, Jonah is being called to empathize with and humanize his enemies.

Yet, when I imagine Jonah setting up camp to overlook what he still likely hoped would be the destruction of Nineveh, I can't help but recall those Israelis who set up viewing parties to overlook and applaud as murderous bombs rain down indiscriminately upon the children, women, and men of Gaza.[2]

I can't help but recall similar stories from Jim Crow America, of families picnicking together at the latest lynching.

I also can't help but recall Nineveh's later importance as a thriving center of Assyrian Christianity, whose reach and influence once outstripped even Rome.

I mourn the destruction of the historic Iraqi Christian community, a direct result of the American invasion of 2003 and resultant ethnic cleansing operations carried out by ISIS after 2014.[3]

It's difficult to imagine how such abject cruelty and dehumanization is possible. Yet, we have seen so much of it in recent years.

In the passage, God is having none of Jonah's petulance and engineers a scenario to highlight his callousness and hypocrisy. As "Jonah accepted God's mercy toward himself [in the fish], but not toward the people of Nineveh," Dr. Emad Boutros writes, "Jonah felt pity for the plant but not for the people."[4]

Such a contrast might seem ridiculous, if not so tragically true to life; dehumanization and demonization lead so easily to violence.

But, as Rev. Naim Ateek explains, "Authentic faith rejects exclusionary forms of religion and places its trust in the one God, creator and Lord of all. Authentic understanding of the people of God rejects exclusionary visions of ethnic superiority and accepts that all people are God's people. Authentic understanding of the land rejects an exclusionary monopoly of one people that involves expulsion and ethnic cleansing and agrees to share the land with the other people of the land on the basis of truth and justice."[5]

This is "the heart of Old Testament theology," an essential internal key for understanding and applying Old Testament Scriptures.

REFLECT

→ Prayerfully read through the verses one more time. Is there a particular word, phrase, or idea that captures your attention?

→ Is there anything new or surprising that you find in the passage? Do you find anything especially challenging?

→ Are you being called to respond or take action in any way?

PRAY

Lord of All Creation, we reject the actions of those who misuse faith to promote hatred, exclusion, and violence. Protect the world from those who seek to undermine diversity and disrupt peace. Empower all people of conscience to speak out against hatred and discrimination, and to defend the universal application of law and the administration of justice.

Lord, in your mercy, hear our prayer.

EXPLORE

A Palestinian Theology of Liberation: The Bible, Justice, and the Palestine-Israel Conflict, by Naim Ateek

See also: "A Palestinian Feminist Reading of the Book of Jonah," by Niveen Sarras

THE BIBLE IS
ANTI-ZIONIST
#39
THE UNITED MONARCHY

THE BIBLE IS ANTI-ZIONIST #39

HERE IS THE ACCOUNT OF THE FORCED LABOUR THAT KING SOLOMON CONSCRIPTED TO BUILD THE HOUSE OF THE LORD AND HIS OWN HOUSE . . . AS WELL AS ALL HIS STORE CITIES AND THE TOWNS FOR HIS CHARIOTS AND FOR HIS HORSES . . . THE WEIGHT OF GOLD THAT CAME TO SOLOMON IN ONE YEAR WAS 666 TALENTS OF GOLD . . . SOLOMON GATHERED TOGETHER CHARIOTS AND HORSES; HE HAD FOURTEEN HUNDRED CHARIOTS AND TWELVE THOUSAND HORSES . . . SOLOMON'S IMPORT OF HORSES WAS FROM EGYPT AND KUE . . . AMONG HIS WIVES WERE SEVEN HUNDRED PRINCESSES AND THREE HUNDRED CONCUBINES.

1 KINGS 9-11 (NIV)

"WHEN YOU HAVE COME INTO THE LAND [AND] YOU SAY, 'I WILL SET A KING OVER ME, **LIKE ALL THE NATIONS** THAT ARE AROUND ME,' YOU MAY INDEED SET OVER YOU A KING . . . EVEN SO, **HE MUST NOT ACQUIRE MANY HORSES** FOR HIMSELF OR **RETURN THE PEOPLE TO EGYPT** IN ORDER TO ACQUIRE MORE HORSES . . . AND HE MUST **NOT ACQUIRE MANY WIVES FOR HIMSELF** OR ELSE HIS HEART WILL TURN AWAY; ALSO **SILVER AND GOLD HE MUST NOT ACQUIRE** IN GREAT QUANTITY FOR HIMSELF.

DUETERONOMY 7:14-16 (NKJV)

The reigns of King David and Solomon, collectively referred to as the United Monarchy, are often looked to as an idealized golden age. Serving as a foundational myth in the identity formation of modern Israel, this era has been used to justify both the establishment of Israel in 1948 and ongoing settler expansion.[1]

The irony, however, is that the biblical text is as deeply critical of the United Monarchy as it would be of the later kings of Judah and Israel. Contrary to popular opinion, Solomon is not a great hero of the faith. When we look to Deuteronomy 7:14-16, we see how King Solomon actually embodies the polar opposite of God's desire as his reign comes to embody the worst excesses of empire and imperial religion.

God delivered the Hebrews from slavery and exploitation in Egypt. Yet, here, in the promised land, the very king who builds the temple has himself become "Pharaoh." (Solomon, by the way, is the literal son-in-law of Pharaoh!)

Therefore, Solomon's apparent success must never be confused with divine blessing, for the book of Kings truly delivers a scathing rebuke of Solomon's so-called golden age:[2]

THE BIBLE IS ANTI-ZIONIST #39

- The fact that the Temple was constructed with slave labor, alongside multiple vanity projects, should give us serious pause.

- To emphasize this point even stronger, in a clear reference to Exodus 1, the text speaks of Solomon "setting up overseers and building storehouses." It's word for word what Pharaoh did to the Hebrew slaves!

- The text even speaks of the establishment of a racialized apartheid regime, of Solomon forcing the Indigenous Canaanites, "the descendants of all these peoples remaining in the land—whom the Israelites could not exterminate—to serve as slave labor" (1 Kings 9:21).

- In addition, we must remember that chariots and horses—all purchased from Egypt—represent the "tanks and warplanes" of the ancient world; these are instruments of imperial conquest. (I can't help but think about Israeli militarism and its dependence, as a client state, on American military support.)

- Finally, seeing 666 as a reference to economic exploitation and wealth extraction is likewise an important corrective to popular apocalyptic misconceptions.

REFLECT

→ Prayerfully read through the verses one more time. Is there a particular word, phrase, or idea that captures your attention?

→ Is there anything new or surprising that you find in the passage? Do you find anything especially challenging?

→ Are you being called to respond or take action in any way?

PRAY

God of Truth, we pray for wisdom and strength for those seeking justice on behalf of the suffering. Guide the hearts and minds of those in power, that they may see clearly and act with fairness and compassion. May the truth bring healing, accountability, and the seeds of peace. We pray for an end to acts of harm and for a world that values each life.

Lord, in your mercy, hear our prayer.

EXPLORE

From Land to Lands, from Eden to the Renewed Earth: A Christ-Centered Biblical Theology of the Promised Land, by Munther Isaac

THE BIBLE IS
ANTI-ZIONIST

#40
SEEK THE PEACE

THE BIBLE IS ANTI-ZIONIST #40

THIS IS WHAT THE LORD ALMIGHTY, THE GOD OF ISRAEL, SAYS TO ALL THOSE I CARRIED INTO EXILE FROM JERUSALEM TO BABYLON:

" BUILD HOUSES AND SETTLE DOWN; PLANT GARDENS AND EAT WHAT THEY PRODUCE. MARRY AND HAVE SONS AND DAUGHTERS; FIND WIVES FOR YOUR SONS AND GIVE YOUR DAUGHTERS IN MARRIAGE, SO THAT THEY TOO MAY HAVE SONS AND DAUGHTERS. INCREASE IN NUMBER THERE; DO NOT DECREASE. ALSO,

SEEK THE PEACE AND PROSPERITY OF THE CITY TO WHICH I HAVE CARRIED YOU INTO EXILE. PRAY TO THE LORD FOR IT, BECAUSE IF IT PROSPERS, YOU TOO WILL PROSPER.

YES, THIS IS WHAT THE LORD ALMIGHTY, THE GOD OF ISRAEL, SAYS: " DO NOT LET THE PROPHETS AND DIVINERS AMONG YOU DECEIVE YOU. DO NOT LISTEN TO THE DREAMS YOU ENCOURAGE THEM TO HAVE. THEY ARE PROPHESYING LIES TO YOU IN MY NAME. I HAVE NOT SENT THEM," DECLARES THE LORD.

JEREMIAH 29:4-9 (NIV)

In his letter to the Judean captives exiled in Babylon, the prophet Jeremiah proclaims: "Seek the peace and prosperity of the city to which I have carried you into exile. Pray to the Lord for it, because if it prospers, you too will prosper."

Themes of exile run through the entirety of Scripture, starting with the primordial exile of our spiritual ancestors Adam and Eve from the Garden of Eden. Abraham, likewise, is a sojourner in a foreign land, as are Jacob and the twelve tribes of Israel. Following their deliverance from slavery in Egypt, the people spent decades wandering the wilderness. Upon entering the "Promised Land," there remained, however, a perpetual feeling that things were incomplete.

In their writings, the biblical historians and prophets focus on the significance of events leading up to, during, and immediately following the Babylonian captivity. Yet, even after returning from exile, rebuilding the Temple, and erecting the walls of Jerusalem, as described in the books of Ezra and Nehemiah, there remained not just a sense of perpetual incompleteness but a sense of perpetual exile. The people would remain under the influence of one violent empire after another. By the time we reach the Gospels, there is a palpable longing for deliverance.

The people, N.T. Wright says, "did not believe that the exile was really, properly over . . . the great promises of Isaiah and Ezekiel hadn't yet come true."[1]

In the Gospels, the theme of exile is consolidated upon the life, death, and resurrection of Jesus Christ. The coming of Jesus, to paraphrase Wright, is presented as God's return to the land, as "the forgiveness of sins" and, therefore, "an end to exile." The coming of the Holy Spirit, first in Jesus and later at Pentecost, was seen as the fulfilment of Old Testament promises. However, as seen in the many parables of Jesus, expectations needed to be managed, and paradigms needed shifting, as "we wait for the full end of exile, for a further coming of, for the New Jerusalem to come down out of heaven to a new heaven and new earth."[2] This is an image of the full and final consummation of the Reign of God, the completed reunification of Heaven and Earth, and the ultimate redemption and reversion of our original exile from the Garden.

Reestablishing a kingdom (or nation-state) like those of the world, let alone one built on settler-colonial violence, would simply repeat the sins of Solomon. Citizenship in "the Holy Nation of Heaven," requires living the way of the Cross. It requires a renunciation of imperial violence and coercive power.

Therefore, as citizens of a kingdom not *from* this world, as "resident aliens," our task is to strive for the peace and prosperity of the land—the world!—into which God has placed us.

Recognizing the Holy Spirit's promise to dwell with us in our sojourn, our exile truly becomes the catalyst for God's redemptive mission to the world via his redeemed people.

Doing so, "we live with the assurance that what has begun so powerfully in Jesus Christ will be completed," Rev. Dr. Marvin Tate explains: "In a sense, all God's people live in exile, waiting for the fulfillment of the promise of God to live in his Presence."[3]

Evoking the Old Testament prophets, the Apostle Peter is led to declare: "You are a chosen race, a royal priesthood, a holy nation, a people who are God's own possession. You have become this people so that you may speak of the wonderful acts of the one who called you out of darkness into his amazing light . . . *Since you are immigrants and strangers in the world,* I urge that you avoid worldly desires that wage war against your lives. Live honorably among the unbelievers. Today, they defame you, as if you were doing evil. But in the day when God visits to judge they will glorify him, because they have observed your honorable deeds" (1 Peter 9-12).

Returning to the words of Jeremiah, we must remember that those false prophets fabricating promises of "imminent return and easy victory over our enemies" must not be heeded. For such posturing, often accompanied by violent claims to land, power, and religious or cultural supremacy, is truly a misguided attempt to force God's hand. So, the Zionist project is not just a pale facsimile, but it is in many respects a total inversion of the biblical vision. As we see in the final pages of Revelation:

> *Then I saw a new heaven and a new earth, for the former heaven and the former earth had passed away, and the sea was no more. I saw the holy city, New Jerusalem, coming down out of heaven from God, made ready as a bride beautifully dressed for her husband.*
>
> *I heard a loud voice from the throne say, "Look! God's dwelling is here with humankind. He will dwell with them, and they will be his peoples. God himself will be with them as their God. He will wipe away every tear from their eyes. Death will be no more. There will be no mourning, crying, or pain anymore, for the former things have passed away"* (Revelation 21:1-4 CEB).

Ultimately, Christian Zionism is a terrible witness to the crucified Christ, a betrayal of our redemptive and emancipatory mission as global citizens of "the Holy Nation of Heaven."

REFLECT

→ Prayerfully read through the verses one more time. Is there a particular word, phrase, or idea that captures your attention?

→ Is there anything new or surprising that you find in the passage? Do you find anything especially challenging?

→ Are you being called to respond or take action in any way?

PRAY

Holy God, we thank you for the chance to bear witness. In times of despair, we still see signs of your love everywhere. Holy Spirit, make us an instrument of your peace and reconciliation. Bless and protect us, so that we may serve as examples for the world. Move our hearts, our minds, and our bodies, so that we may serve where we are most needed.

Lord, in your mercy, hear our prayer.

EXPLORE

How God Became King: The Forgotten Story of the Gospels, by N.T. Wright

THE BIBLE IS ANTI-ZIONIST

POSTSCRIPT: APOLOGIA

On the 14th of May 2018, the United States controversially broke with decades of US policy by officially moving its embassy from Tel Aviv to Jerusalem, followed soon after by Guatemala, Paraguay, and Honduras. Meanwhile, thousands of Gazans continued to engage nonviolently in ongoing demonstrations at the separation barrier, as part of the Great March of Return, while Israeli military snipers responded with lethal force, leading on that day to the death of 64 persons.

The split screen coverage contrasting the elegance of the embassy opening in Jerusalem with that of the carnage in Gaza set forth a dramatic scene, one Israeli commentator comparing it to Charles Dickens' *A Tale of Two Cities*.

Of noteworthy importance, however, is the bit of trivia concerning who was—and who was not—on the guest and speaker list of the embassy opening. In addition to the expected list of diplomats, dignitaries, and political donors, one finds an assortment of prominent American pastors and religious leaders.

Particularly emblematic were the names and profiles of those invited to give the benediction and closing prayer: Revs. Robert Jeffress and John Hagee, each the author of multiple books about Israel and the impending apocalypse. Mainstream Jewish leaders, however, were not invited, nor were Catholic, Orthodox, or Mainline Protestant representatives in attendance.

The inclusion of Jeffress and Hagee speaks volumes as to the purpose behind and intended audience for the embassy opening. This event taking place in Jerusalem was not meant for Israelis, nor even American Jews.

Instead, it was clearly meant for the American evangelical voter, Trump's most consistent base of political support. Given the fact that 81% of white American evangelicals voted for Trump and have remained his most reliable political supporters, while other demographics have waned, this is not surprising. Allegiance to Israel has long been a point of doctrine among these communities, with 80% of American Evangelicals at the time viewing Israel as the fulfillment of Biblical prophecy.

Because Christian Zionists in America outnumber Jewish Zionists ten-to-one, the presence of Jeffress and Hagee onstage is not surprising—even as both have been accused of making proclamations deeply offensive to Jews.

What effectively unfolded on our screen was an apocalyptic drama, broadcast in real-time and orchestrated largely for a conservative Christian audience. Such viewers were able to consume events of "eternal, apocalyptic significance" vicariously, from the safety of their television and computer screens.

While the split screen contrast between Jerusalem and Gaza led many to recoil in disgust at the apparent callousness of the historical moment, for others it was all part of the show—an event further cementing Israel's status as an "evangelical Disneyland."

Every drama needs a villain, and if there is anything Hollywood cinema has taught us, it is that "real bad Arabs" make for great villains.[1] It was simply more proof in the eyes of the viewing public that "the 'enemies of God' will continue to rage against his purposes and his people."

The situation represented yet another instance of American foreign policy being influenced by domestic political agendas and homegrown pop-theologies projected out upon the global stage by means of US political, commercial, and military influence.

It represents a false matrix of meaning blanketed over the region without thought or concern as to how such views may or may not reflect historical reality or how the policy ramifications of such beliefs affect people on the ground—be they Israeli, Palestinian, Christian, Muslim, Jewish, or otherwise. To what extent such theologizing may or may not be consistent with Scripture is never asked.[2]

But, as I shared in the Introduction, if we are people committed to the truth, like we so often claim, then we must engage with the witness of both Scripture and history honestly and with open hearts, ready to be formed into the disciples God desires us to be.

In conclusion, I wish to respond to an anticipated criticism from those compelled to ask what authority I have, as a non-Jewish, white American Evangelical Christian, to speak about Zionism. To me, the answer is simple:

1. Contrary to popular belief, Christian Zionists outnumber Jewish Zionists ten-to-one. As such, the political calculus of American support for Israel is built to a large extent on the strength of a wealthy and incredibly powerful Christian Zionist voting block.[3]

2. Christian Zionism predates Jewish Zionism, even influencing the growth and expansion of the Zionist movement itself. The influence of Christian Zionist thought on British imperial policy at the turn of and into the 20th century is well documented.[4]

3. Zionism has been a Christian and western imperial project as much as it has been a Jewish project. Therefore, to lay the blame for Zionist violence at the feet of Jews alone would be as antisemitic as many of the worst accusations and abuses of the past. Moreover, if not for the severe persecution of Jews by Christians in the West, the felt need for "a Jewish homeland" would likely never have been as strong. Blame belongs everywhere blame is due.

4. After two years of live-streamed genocide in Gaza and severe ethnic cleansing in the West Bank (following decades of brutal apartheid), there are no excuses for remaining silent. Everyone has a moral obligation to speak out and act! All complicit leaders and institutions must be confronted, be they Christian, Jewish, Muslim, secular, or any other. All industries who profit from the dispossession or death of another must be held to account, be they technological, financial, military, or any other.

5. The Palestinian people have asked me to. As the silenced victims of Zionism, it is their voices and experiences we must center and amplify, and with whom we must stand in costly solidarity. This often means "running interference" as a protective presence and speaking boldly and prophetically to our own communities.

As ***Kairos Palestine II - A Moment of Truth: Faith in a Time of Genocide***[5] (launched November 2025) declares:

We reject the oppression and injustice produced by the theology of racism, colonialism and ethnic supremacy embodied in Christian Zionism, a theology that has produced apartheid, ethnic cleansing, and genocide of indigenous people.

Christian Zionism calls on a tribal, racist god of war and ethnic cleansing, teachings utterly alien to the core of Christian faith and ethics. Christian Zionism must therefore be named for what it is: a theological and moral corruption.

After all efforts to invite Christian Zionists to genuine repentance have been exhausted, moral, ecclesial and theological responsibility requires that they be held accountable and that their ideology be rejected and boycotted.

The time has come for the churches of the world to repudiate Zionist theology and to state clearly their position on Palestine: this is a case of settler colonialism and ethnic cleansing of an indigenous people.

ENDNOTES

Introduction

1. Jesse Steven Wheeler, "Bad Theology Kills: How We Justify Killing Arabs," in Keeping the Faith: Reflections on Politics & Christianity in the Era of Trump & Beyond, (KTF Press, 2020). See also: Jesse S. Wheeler, "Bad Theology Kills: How We Justify Killing Arabs," The ABTS Blog, April 17, 2024, https://abtslebanon.org/2014/04/17/bad-theology-kills-how-we-justify-killing-arabs/.
2. Anne Perez, *Understanding Zionism: History and Perspectives* (Fortress Press, 2023).
3. Jesse Steven Wheeler, "Zionism Is What Zionism Does": Personal Encounters with Zionism," *Washington Report on Middle East Affairs*, May 25, 2025, https://www.wrmea.org/israel-palestine/zionism-is-what-zionism-does-personal-encounters-with-zionism.html.
4. Glen H. Stassen, "Critical Thinking and Prophetic Witness, Historically–Theologically Based," Religion Studies News, March 2008, http://rsnonline.org/indexc6fd.html?option=com_content&view=article&id=262:critical-thinking-and-prophetic-witness-historicallytheologically-based&catid=25:spotlight-on-theo-educ&Itemid=343.
5. "A Moment of Truth: Faith in a Time of Genocide," Kairos Palestine – The Palestinian Christian Initiative, November 14, 2025, https://kairospalestine.ps/index.php/about-kairos/kairos-palestine-ii.
6. "Wave of Prayer," Sabeel Ecumenical Liberation Theology Centre, https://sabeel.org/wave-of-prayers/.

#2 - Whose Land?

1. Al-Jazeera, "Israel's Netanyahu says 'there will be no Palestinian state,'" September 11, 2025. https://www.aljazeera.com/news/2025/9/11/israels-netanyahu-says-there-will-be-no-palestinian-state#:~:text=Israeli%20prime%20minister%20signs%20agreement,1%E2%80%9D%20or%20%E2%80%9CE1%E2%80%9D.

2. The *Jerusalem Post*, "Israeli ambassador's 'Bible speech' at U.N. goes viral," May 18, 2019. https://www.jpost.com/diaspora/israeli-ambassadors-bible-speech-at-un-goes-viral-589986
3. *Al-Jazeera*, "What is Greater Israel, and how popular is it among Israelis?" February 26, 2026, https://www.aljazeera.com/news/2026/2/26/what-is-greater-israel-and-how-popular-is-it-among-israelis.
4. *Elias Chacour, We Belong to the Land: The Story of a Palestinian Israeli Who Lives for Peace and Reconciliation* (University of Notre Dame Press, 2021).

#3 - The Indigenous Other

1. *Mitri Raheb, Decolonizing Palestine: The Land, The People, The Bible* (Orbis Books, 2023), 20.
2. Raheb, *Decolonizing*, 8.

#4 - Native Born

1. @MiddleEastEye, "Historian says Palestine word as old as literacy itself," August 17, 2025, https://www.youtube.com/shorts/BkNdx8deU9Y
2. William Dalrymple (@DalrympleWill), X.com, September 13, 2025, https://x.com/DalrympleWill/status/19669445186721837 56

#5 - The World & Everything in It

1. Mersiha Gadzo, "What do Texan red heifers have to do with Al-Aqsa and a Jewish temple?" April 9, 2024, https://www.aljazeera.com/news/2024/4/9/what-do-texan-red-heifers-have-to-do-with-al-aqsa-and-a-jewish-temple.
2. Colin Chapman, *Whose Holy City: Jerusalem and the Future of Peace in the Middle East* (Lion Books, 2004), 25.

ENDNOTES

#6 - What Zionism Does

1. Wheeler, "Zionism Is."
2. "Statistics on House / Structure Demolitions – November 1947-February 2026," ICAHD, April 26, 20211 (updated February 2026), https://icahd.org/2021/04/26/statistics-on-house-structure-demolitions-november-1947/
3. See: www.targetedchurches.com. Also: Tobias Holcman, "Smotrich, Sa'ar approve NIS 2.35 billion in hasbara budget for campaigns, influencers in 2026," *The Jerusalem Post*, December 6, 2025, https://www.jpost.com/israel-news/politics-and-diplomacy/article-879369.
4. Glen H. Stassen, "Critical Thinking and Prophetic Witness, Historically–Theologically Based," *Religion Studies News*, March 2008, http://rsnonline.org/indexc6fd.html?option=com_content&view=article&id=262:critical-thinking-and-prophetic-witness-historicallytheologically-based&catid=25:spotlight-on-theo-educ&Itemid=343.

#7 - Reeds & Branches

1. Jewish Voice for Peace (@JewishVoiceforPeace), "What Is Zionism?" November 28, 2023, https://www.facebook.com/jewishvoiceforpeace/posts/were-proud-anti-zionists-at-jvp-but-what-is-zionism-and-why-are-we-opposed-to-it/756785769824925/
2. Raheb, "Decolonizing," 54-55.
3. "On Antisemitism, Anti-Zionism and Dangerous Conflations," *Jewish Voice for Peace*, November 9, 2023, https://www.jewishvoiceforpeace.org/2023/11/09/antisemitism-dangerous/.

#8 - Blessings & Curses

1. Noureldein Ghanem, "Genesis 12:3 — The Bible verse that far-right Americans misinterpret to defend Israel," *TRT World*, July 23, 2025, https://www.trtworld.com/article/5081f8ade0cf.
2. Ghanem, "Genesis 12."

ENDNOTES

#9 - Children of Abraham

1. Ghanem, "Genesis 12."
2. Ghanem, "Genesis 12."

#11 - The Temple

1. See: N.T. Wright, *The New Testament and the People of God* (Fortress Press, 1992).
2. Britannica Editors. "Rabbinic Judaism." Encyclopedia Britannica, February 19, 2025. https://www.britannica.com/topic/Rabbinic-Judaism.
3. Ida Glaser, *Thinking Biblically about Islam: Genesis, Transfiguration, Transformation* (Langham Global Library, 2016), 268.

#12 - Countless Crimes

1. Mark Wingfield, "'We are on the side of God,' Stephen Miller says," *Baptist News Global*, September 22, 2025, https://baptistnews.com/article/we-are-on-the-side-of-god-stephen-miller-says/.
2. "Statements by PM Netanyahu and US Secretary of State Marco Rubio," Israeli Ministry of Foreign Affairs, September 15, 2025, https://www.gov.il/en/pages/statements-by-pm-netanyahu-and-us-secretary-of-state-marco-rubio-15-sep-2025.
3. *The Guardian*, "Israel minister condemned for saying starvation of millions in Gaza might be 'justified and moral,'" August 7, 2024, https://www.theguardian.com/world/article/2024/aug/08/israel-finance-minister-bezalel-smotrich-gaza-starve-2m-people-comments#:~:text=Bezalel%20Smotrich%2C%20Israel%27s%20far%2Dright,order%20to%20free%20the%20hostages.%E2%80%9D.
4. Image credit: https://tinyurl.com/u3j3ac7h.

ENDNOTES

#13 - Choose Good

1. Daryl P. Domning, "How Should the People and the Land of Israel be Understood in the Light of the Covenant?" in *Zionism through Christian Lenses: Ecumenical Perspectives on the Promised Land*, ed. Carole Monica Burnett (Pickwick Publications, 2013), 6.

#14 - Oceans of Justice

1. Jewish Voice for Peace (@JewishVoiceforPeace), "This Is Zionism," Facebook, September 26, 2025, https://www.facebook.com/jewishvoiceforpeace/posts/we-are-appalled-yet-unsurprised-to-see-israeli-soldiers-celebrating-the-jewish-n/1237542395082591/.

#15 - No Less Important

1. N.T. Wright, *How God Became King: The Forgotten Story of the Gospels* (HarperOne, 2026), 73.

#16 - A Strange Anticlimax

1. Colin Chapman, *Christian Zionism and the Restoration of Israel: How Should We Interpret the Scriptures?* (Cascade Books, 2021), 81.
2. Chapman, *Christian Zionism*, 83

#17 - Declared Clean

1. Anton Deik, "Christian Zionism and Mission: How Does Our Understanding of Christianity Impact Our Witness in the World?" in *The Religious Other: A Biblical Understanding of Islam, the Qur'an and Muhammad*, ed. Martin Accad and Jonathan Andrews (Langham Global Library, 2020), 108.
2. Deik, "Mission," 113.
3. Deik, "Mission," 113-114.
4. Deik, "Mission," 114.
5. Deik, "Mission," 116.

#18 - Staring at Clouds

1. Chapman, *Christian Zionism*, 116.
2. As quoted in: Chapman, Christian Zionism, 117.

#19 - Dispossession

1. For a phenomenal historical survey of the region, see: Eugene Rogan, *The Arabs: A History, rev. ed.* (Basic Books, 2017).
2. *TRT World*, "Israel grants gas exploration licenses within Palestine's maritime boundary," February 15, 2024, https://www.trtworld.com/article/16994332.
3. Walter Brueggemann, "What Naboth Teaches Us Today (Part I)," *Church Anew*, January 22, 2021, https://churchanew.org/brueggemann/what-naboth-teaches-us-today-part-i.
4. Brueggemann, "Naboth."

#20 - Sumud

1. "Palestinian Culture," Anera, March 22, 2021, https://www.anera.org/blog/palestinian-culture/.
2. *Handala Foundation*, "Why Palestinians Stay: The Deep Connection Between Land, Identity and Survival," October 6 2025, https://www.handalafoundation.nl/nieuws/why-palestinians-stay-the-deep-connection-between-land-identity-and-survival.
3. Handala, "Deep Connection."
4. Handala, "Deep Connection."

#21 - Peace. Joy. Liberation.

1. John S. Munayer and Samual S. Munayer, "Introduciton," in The Cross and the Olive Tree: Cultivating Palestinian Theology amid Gaza, ed. John S. Munayer and Samuel S. Munayer (Orbis Books, 2025), xvi.

2. Alex Awad, "Colliding Forces during the Christmas Season," *The FOSNA Blog*, November 20, 2021, https://www.fosna.org/preach-palestine-blog/colliding-forces-during-the-christmas-season.
3. Awad, "Forces."
4. Frederick Clarkson and Ben Lorber, "The New Face of Christian Zionism," *In These Times*, March 31, 2025, https://inthesetimes.com/article/christian-zionism-evangelicals-right-wing-israel-palestine.
5. Robert O. Smith, "Gaza and the Christian Zionist Present," *Journal for the Study of Christian Zionism* 1 no. 2 (2026): 13, https://studychristianzionism.org/wp-content/uploads/2026/01/Smith.pdf.

#22 - Paternalism

1. See: Wheeler, "Bad Theology Kills."
2. Brian McLaren, "Post-Colonial Theology," *Sojourners*, September 15, 2010, https://sojo.net/articles/post-colonial-theology.

#23 - Crusaderism

1. See: Wheeler, "Bad Theology Kills."
2. Joseph Cumming, "Toward Respectful Witness," in *Seed to Fruit: Global Trends, Fruitful Practices and Emerging Issues among Muslims*, J. Dudley Woodberry, ed. (William Carey Library, 2009), 320.
3. The *Times of Israel*, "Netanyahu transcript: 'We have to be more powerful than the barbarians, or they will crash our gates, destroy our societies,'" March 20, 2026, https://www.timesofisrael.com/netanyahu-transcript-we-have-to-be-more-powerful-than-the-barbarians-or-they-will-crash-our-gates-destroy-our-societies/.

#24 - Manifest Destiny

1. See: Wheeler, "Bad Theology Kills."
2. Raheb, *Decolonizing*, 20.

3. Chapman, "A Biblical Perspective on Israel/Palestine" in *The Land Cries Out: Theology of the Land in the Israeli/Palestinian Context*, eds. Salim Munayer and Lisa Loden (Wipf and Stock Publisher, 2012), 238.

#25 - The God Who Sees

1. Havilah Dharamraj, "Do You See What I See: The Story of Hagar," in The Religious Other: A Biblical Understanding of Islam, the Qur'an and Muhammad, ed. Martin Accad and Jonathan Andrews (Langham Global Library, 2020), 79.
2. Dharamraj, "Hagar," 78.

#26 - Resident Aliens

1. John Goldingay, *Genesis, for Everyone, Part 2* (Westminster John Knox Press, 2010), 365.
2. Dharamraj, "Hagar," 74.
3. Dharamraj, "Hagar," 75.

#27 - Refusing Silence

1. Kenneth E. Bailey, *Jesus Through Middle Eastern Eyes: Cultural Studies in the Gospels* (IVP Academic, 2008), 41.
2. Calligraphy by Dr. Wageeh Mikhail, https://www.facebook.com/photo.php?fbid=679080529101578l&set=pb.100002591327063.-2207520000&type=3.

#28 - Refusing False Comfort

1. Bailey, Jesus, 56-58.

#29 - A Story of Empire

1. Ida Glaser, *The Bible and Other Faiths: What Does the Lord Require of Us?* (Langham Global Library, 2012), 80-82.
2. Glaser, Other Faiths, 80.
3. Glaser, Other Faiths, 81.
4. Glaser, Other Faiths, 81.
5. Glaser, Other Faiths, 82.

#30 - Should You Inherit the Land?

1. *Middle East Monitor*, "Israel declares it is above the law," September 21, 2018, https://www.middleeastmonitor.com/20180921-israel-declares-it-is-above-the-law/.
2. Stephen Sizer, "Seven Biblical Answers to Popular Zionist Assumptions," 2nd ed., StephenSizer.com, January 2014, https://www.fosna.org/s/7answers.pdf
3. Sizer, "7 Answers."
4. "Israel's assault on the foundations of international law must have consequences: UN experts," United Nations Human Rights Office of the High Commissioner, December 30, 2024, https://www.ohchr.org/en/press-releases/2024/12/israels-assault-foundations-international-law-must-have-consequences-un.

#31 - The Rapture Does Not Exist

1. Sizer, "7 Answers."
2. Jonathan Larsen, "U.S. Troops Were Told Iran War Is for 'Armageddon,' Return of Jesus," *Jonathan Larsen's Substack*, March 02, 2026, https://jonathanlarsen.substack.com/p/us-troops-were-told-iran-war-is-for.
3. Wright, *Jesus*, 200.

#32 - Disturbing the Peace

1. Wright, *People of God*, 450.

#33 - For all peoples

1. "H5236 - nēḵār - Strong's Hebrew Lexicon (KJV)." Blue Letter Bible. Accessed 8 Mar, 2026. https://www.blueletterbible.org/lexicon/h5236/kjv/wlc/0-1/.
2. Sizer, "7 Answers."

#34 - Hometown Hero

1. Naim Ateek, "Today the Scripture is Fulfilled," in *The Bible and the Palestine-Israel Conflict* (Sabeel, 2014), 31-37.

2. Wright, *People of God*, 451.

#35 - You Have Heard It Said

1. Brian Kaylor, **"A Call for 'Biblical' Genocide,"** Word & Way, October 21, 2023, https://wordandway.org/2023/10/31/a-call-for-biblical-genocide/.
2. See: Sarojini Nadar, *Gender, Genocide, Gaza and the Book of Esther: Engaging Texts of Terror(ism)* (Routledge, 2025).
3. See: Glen H. Stassen, *Living the Sermon on the Mount: A Practical Hope for Grace and Deliverance* (Jossey-Bass, 2006).

#36 - Love Your Enemies

1. Raheb, *Decolonizing*, 88.
2. Raheb, Decolonizing, 88.
3. Raheb, Decolonizing, 90.
4. "Hope for Peace" Monument by artist Armand Fernandez, https://commons.wikimedia.org/wiki/File:Lebanon_tank_monument.jpg.

#37 - Neither Us, Nor Our Enemies

1. Raheb, *Decolonizing*, 90
2. See: "The Book of Joshua," Bible Project Guide, *The Bible Project*, https://bibleproject.com/guides/book-of-joshua/.
3. Glaser, *Other Faiths*, 85-86.

#38 - Empathy & Repentance

1. Naim Ateek, *A Palestinian Theology of Liberation: The Bible, Justice, and the Palestine-Israel Conflict*, 76-82.
2. Lucas Minisini, "'The best show in town': From a hilltop in Israel, observers have a sinister view of Gaza bombings," *Le Monde*, July 23, 2025, https://www.lemonde.fr/en/international/article/2025/07/23/the-best-show-in-town-from-a-hilltop-in-israel-observers-have-a-sinister-view-of-gaza-bombings_6743627_4.html.

3. The Associated Press, "A timeline of disaster and displacement for Iraqi Christians," March 5, 2021, https://apnews.com/article/middle-east-islamic-state-group-saddam-hussein-baghdad-iraq-296b5588995cf7be62b49619bf1a7bb6. See also: Ramazan Kılınç, "Pope's upcoming visit brings attention to the dwindling population of Christians in Iraq," *The Conversation*, March 3, 2021, https://theconversation.com/popes-upcoming-visit-brings-attention-to-the-dwindling-population-of-christians-in-iraq-152421.
4. Emad Boutros, "Jonah: An Encounter with God in the School of Creation," in *The Religious Other: A Biblical Understanding of Islam, the Qur'an and Muhammad* (Langham Global Library, 2020), 29.
5. Ateek, *Liberation*, 82.

#39 - The United Monarchy

1. Raheb, *Decolonizing*, 85.
2. Tim Mackie, "Solomon: Love Him or Hate Him?" *The Bible Project*, April 2, 2017, https://bibleproject.com/articles/solomon-love-hate/.

#40 - Seek the Peace

1. Wright, *King*, 69.
2. Marvin E. Tate, *From Promise to Exile: The Former Prophets* (Smyth & Helwys, 1999), 120.
3. Tate, *Promise*, 120.

Postscript

1. Jack G. Shaheen, Reel Bad Arabs: How Hollywood Vilifies a People (Olive Branch Press, 2012). See also: https://www.youtube.com/watch?v=TPxak6lFd-I.
2. Jesse Steven Wheeler, "Palestine/Israel" The IMES Regional Brief, June 2018, https://abtslebanon.org/palestine-israel-brief-june-2018/.

3. Daniel Hummel, "White evangelical Christians are some of Israel's biggest supporters. Why?" interview by Gene Demby, *Code Switch*, NPR, May 29, 2024, https://www.npr.org/transcripts/1197956512.
4. Stephen Sizer, "Christian Zionism and the Church of England: Historic Beginnings," *Journal for the Study of Christian Zionism* Volume 1, no. 1 (2025), 2-22, https://studychristianzionism.org/the-journal-for-the-study-of-christian-zionism-volume-1-no-1/.
5. Kairos Palestine, "A Moment of Truth: Faith in a Time of Genocide."

THANK YOU

www.ingramcontent.com/pod-product-compliance
Lightning Source LLC
LaVergne TN
LVHW010854110826
845149LV00005B/1404

9798994929742